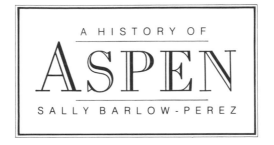

A HISTORY OF

ASPEN

SALLY BARLOW-PEREZ

Second Edition

WHO PRESS · BASALT, COLORADO

PUBLISHED BY

WHO Press
www.whopress.com

Library of Congress Catalog Card Number: 99-75721

ISBN 1-882426-14-2

Second Edition 2000

Printed in the United States of America

PHOTOGRAPHIC CREDITS

Aspen Historical Society pp. 6-7, 9-10, 14-17, 19-21, 23, 25-26, 28, 30, 32-33, 35-42, 47-49, 53, 55, 56(top), 58, 71, 76-80

Michael Brands/*The Aspen Times* pp. 83-84, 86, 90, 94, 96, 99

Frank Martin pp. 65-66, 85, 88, 93, 101(middle), 102(top)

Ferenc Berko pp. 51-52, 56(bottom), 61, 63, 72

Mary Eshbaugh Hayes pp. 92, 97, 101(bottom)

Margaret Durrance pp. 44-45, 50, 54, 59-60

Chris Cassatt pp. 69-70, 81, 102(bottom)

Bob Chamberlain pp. 64, 74-75, 103

Aspen Music Festival p. 101(top)

Colorado Historical Society p. 4

Lou Dawson p. 67

Book Design by Curt Carpenter

Edited by Warren H. Ohlrich

Table of Contents

Ute Indians photographed by William Henry Jackson

The Mining Era: 1879–1893

The year was 1879 when Aspen's first real prospectors carefully inched their way down the steep slopes of Hunter's Pass—soon to be known as Independence Pass—following the rushing waters that the Ute Indians called Thunder River. The Civil War had been over for fifteen years. The great movement west had already replaced the hardy mountain men and fur traders with families of ranchers and farmers. The Indians, including the region's native Utes, had been relegated to reservations. The transcontinental railroad was ten years old and the state of Colorado was three years old. Alexander Graham Bell and Thomas Edison had just patented discoveries that would revolutionize society. But it was other discoveries that led these explorers and hundreds of others into the most isolated corners of the mountains: that of gold, silver, copper, and lead. America was in the midst of four decades of unprecedented mineral exploration.

The California Gold Rush in 1848 set the stage. In 1859, after half a century of rumors from Indians, explorers, and traders about mineral riches, gold was discovered in Colorado. One hundred thousand miners rushed to the Rockies, founding Denver and finding pockets of gold in the mountains above. That year the rich Comstock Lode was discovered in Virginia City, Nevada. In the twenty years between 1860 and 1880, $300,000,000 worth of gold and silver came from the Comstock Lode. In the process, its miners developed the technology that would be essential in the development of Colorado's Western Slope.

Aspen's First Arrivals

Aspen's early prospectors were almost all from Leadville, where in 1877, after years of disappointing gold mining, rich silver deposits were found. Just three years after the strikes, Leadville had a population of over 15,000, making it Colorado's second largest city. In 1879 over $9 million in silver was mined in Leadville. But for every strike, there were hundreds of barren claims. As one weary miner said, "I never worked so hard in my life to get rich without working."

Leadville teemed with entrepreneurs looking for newer, richer pastures. So when Frederick V. Hayden's *Atlas of Colorado* was published, at least two groups found a good reason to explore the surrounding territory. The *Atlas* was the result of Hayden's 1873 State Commission to map the geologic and topographic features of Colorado with a surveying crew.

The Hayden survey crew in 1873

In Leadville, prospectors had learned that geological formations could reveal information about hidden mineral deposits. So when Hayden's survey fell into the hands of two Leadville-based mining entrepreneurs, Charles E. Bennett and Philip W. Pratt, both noticed that formations similar to those of Leadville existed in the valley just to the southwest. They hoped that the silver veins that existed in Leadville might extend right through the mountain range into the neighboring valley.

Although Chief Ouray had given Hayden permission to survey the Roaring Fork Valley, the would-be prospectors had to wait nearly a year for a treaty with the Utes to permit exploration and settlement. Finally, in 1879, unbeknownst to one another, both Bennett and Pratt formed exploring parties and set off for the Roaring Fork Valley at the height of Colorado's short alpine summer.

Even in summer, the 72-mile trip from Leadville to the Roaring Fork Valley would have been an arduous journey. Riding on horseback and leading pack horses, the parties would have made their way south to Granite and then gradually upward past Twin Lakes. Both groups must have known that they were among the first white people ever to tread the foothills above the lakes. Perhaps they traveled on paths generated by Indians or animals; or perhaps they found no tracks at all along the marshy tundra below the pass. But summer travelers approaching Aspen from the south today may stop and imagine the awesome task of those first prospectors, cautiously ascending fifteen miles of steep mountain to the chill 12,095-foot summit of Independence Pass.

Philip Pratt, accompanied by Smith Steele and William L. Hopkins, passed this way during the last week in June. The Bennett party— which included Walter S. Clark, A. C. Fellows, and S. E. Hopkins— is said to have spent the night of July 4, 1879, on the pass.

They started downward at dawn. The 20-mile trip from the summit must have looked even more daunting to the prospectors zigzagging among the huge boulders with horses in hand, looking for unfriendly Utes and at the same time keeping a sharp eye out for the geologic formations that brought them on this dangerous journey. Following the rushing Roaring Fork River, they saw much of what we see today: a misty gap in the mountains about halfway down; the lovely "still waters" and marshy wetlands at the east end of the valley; a northward curve of the river; and the firm, wide valley floor between the mountains. The landmark mountains have not changed: Aspen Mountain and Shadow Mountain (first called West Aspen Mountain) on the south, and the gentler rises of Smuggler Mountain, Red Mountain (first called Pratt Mountain), and Red Butte on the north.

Perhaps these experienced prospectors made instant comparisons with the Hayden surveys as they rode through the valley, calling excitedly to one another as they saw the remarkably promising outcroppings of rock. Progressing onward down the valley, the Bennett party rode close to Aspen Mountain, crossed Castle and Maroon creeks, and there, where the Buttermilk Ski Area now is, were surprised by Pratt and his companions.

The Pratt party had already been exploring for a week and had staked out several claims, including what would be the Spar and the Galena (sometimes called the Pioneer), both on Aspen Mountain. But it was soon agreed that there were enough mineral riches in the area for all of them. The two parties camped together in the meadows and no doubt whiled away the evening with visions of the silver buried in the surrounding peaks.

The miners at the Durant pose for the camera

The Pratt party left the next morning, and the four remaining prospectors set to work staking out eight major claims: the Durant, the One-Thousand-and-One, the Monarch, the Iron, the Hopkins, and the Mose on Aspen Mountain; the Steele on Shadow Mountain; and the

Smuggler on Smuggler Mountain. Some accounts say that a lone prospector named Fuller had actually claimed the Smuggler as the Arkansas earlier, but never made the necessary improvements. Bennett also staked out two ranch claims covering the area that later became the site of the town. Although Bennett, Clark, Fellows, and Hopkins only stayed for five days, they accomplished a great deal. Mining statutes demanded that each claim be staked in a rectangle of 1,500 feet by 300 feet. Then, in order to keep the claims, it was necessary to do at least $100 worth of work every year. So the men may have sunk ten-foot shafts for each claim. Some reports indicate that the party built the city's first log cabin which remained standing for many years.

In any case, Bennett, Clark, Hopkins, and Fellows were sure they had found a bonanza. It is easy to imagine their euphoria as they rode towards the pass and headed for Leadville to register their claims with the county clerk in the Lake County Courthouse. It did not take long for word of the new discoveries to spread. Pratt and Bennett were confident that they had staked out the best of the outcroppings and probably made no secret of it. New possibilities were always on everyone's lips, and the Roaring Fork Valley quickly became the focus of many a prospector's dreams.

From Leadville there were three major routes into the Roaring Fork Valley: south to Granite and then up through Twin Lakes and over Independence Pass; south to Buena Vista and then through Cottonwood, over the Continental Divide via Cottonwood Pass and Taylor Pass, and then down into the Roaring Fork Valley through Ashcroft; or north from Leadville and over the Continental Divide via Tennessee Pass, then westward along the Colorado River (then called the Grand), and finally up the Roaring Fork River past what are now Glenwood Springs and Basalt.

Within sixty days of Bennett's and Pratt's explorations, dozens of prospectors and suppliers found their way to the new diggings. Many of the prospectors had been grubstaked by Leadville entrepreneurs in search of fresh opportunities. But while the would-be silver miners crawled up and down the crevices of the area's mountains, the neighboring Utes grew restless. Angry at the latest intrusions into their territory, a party of Indians left the Ute reservation and on September 29, 1879, murdered the Indian Agent Nathan Meeker and eleven associates at the White River Agency 100 miles northwest of the camp. Governor Frederick Pitkin quickly dispatched a messenger to the camp on the Roaring Fork with warnings about a possible uprising. As a result, a majority of the new arrivals lost no time in departing for safer territory. About thirty-five people were left behind to spend the winter. Among them was Warner A. Root, who quit his job as a reporter for the *Daily Eclipse* in Leadville, joined four other adventurers in

November 1879 and began the journey over Independence Pass to the new mining camp.

"All in all," he said, " it was not to be compared to a ride to grandfather's farm in a New England Thanksgiving time. The emergency features which might appear in a tenderfoot's first trip across the snowy range could but illy compensate for the mishaps and adventures which befell us on our way."

By then the area had been christened Ute City by an entrepreneur who was to have a lasting effect on the fledgling city: Henry B. Gillespie.

Henry B. Gillespie

The Early Pioneers

Henry Gillespie was a native of Missouri and a graduate of Kansas State University. In 1874 he settled in Boulder, Colorado, and became a bookkeeper for Abel D. Breed, a Cincinnati businessman who made his fortune in patent medicines and coffins, and had mining interests in Boulder's Caribou mines. Some years later the restless Gillespie succumbed to the lure of Leadville where he opened a downtown office. He hoped to be one of those who profited from new discoveries by using his own wits and someone else's money. When he heard the news about Philip Pratt's claims on the Roaring Fork River, he saw his chance. He moved swiftly to buy options on the Spar and the Galena from Philip Pratt, agreeing to pay the asking price, $25,000, at a later date. All this Gillespie did on the basis of Pratt's enthusiasm and his own intuition. Not a single ounce of ore backed up the assumption that silver lay beneath Aspen Mountain's craggy rock.

Nevertheless, Gillespie was confident enough to persuade a number of miners to travel with him to the camp and begin developing his properties. By now it was fall and the passes were already snowy. The party—including W. E. Koch, who was later the postmaster, and his son—had to make part of the journey on snowshoes. Once there, Gillespie set to work organizing the dozen or so prospectors who had survived the Indian scare and settled in for the winter. Perhaps Gillespie was the leader they were waiting for. They made no protest when he brought them together for a meeting, named the site Ute City, and had the prospectors sign a petition requesting a post office from the federal government. For the struggling prospectors, he painted a bright picture of Ute City's future, complete with a telegraph,

9

a post office, paved streets, railroads, and prosperity. Then, promising to return soon, he departed for the East.

Gillespie went first to Cincinnati where he persuaded his old employer, Abel Breed, to buy a half interest in his new Ute City holdings. Next he traveled to Washington D.C. with the petition for the post office and, finally, he went on to Philadelphia where he persuaded a group of investors to form the Roaring Fork Improvement Company. The purpose of the company was to provide amenities for the new community and, at the same time, profit from them.

Meanwhile, in the remote mining town supposedly isolated by the winter snows, a dynamo known as the "professor" was making things happen.

B. Clark Wheeler was a native of Tioga, Pennsylvania. Trained as a teacher, he served as a principal of several high schools before he studied law and, in 1864, departed for the West. He made the Rockies, from Canada to Mexico, his stomping grounds, frequenting the mining camps and soaking up enough knowledge to call himself a mining engineer. In

B. Clark Wheeler

fact, his true calling was that of a promoter with boundless energy and optimism.

November 1879 found Wheeler variously in Leadville and Denver, generally at loose ends and looking for an interesting proposition. He found it in the rumors of the new camp on the Roaring Fork and in a chance meeting with a young Cincinnati accountant named Charles Hallam. Hallam had come west seeking adventure and had brought with him a directive from his friend David Hyman to be on the lookout for an interesting investment involving as much as $5,000.

Denver was ablaze with talk of mining investments. Wheeler told his new friend of the wonderful opportunities available in Ute City. Together the two traveled to Leadville to talk to prospectors who had been to the Roaring Fork camp. Promising reports of the camp, along with the optimism and excitement that filled Leadville, were all that it took to convince Hallam. He cabled Hyman that he had found his investment. When Hyman received the details by mail, he was stunned to learn that instead of the agreed upon $5,000, he had been obligated for a total of $165,000. The deal involved the purchase of seven-and-a-half of the eight mining claims, plus the two ranch claims filed by Charles Bennett and his party. The conservative Ohio attorney, who had never been west of the Mississippi, left at once for Leadville to assess the situation.

Once there, amidst the seductive bustle of Leadville, Hyman conferred with Hallam and with the colorful B. Clark Wheeler. No two men could have been more different: the successful Edwardian attorney and the flamboyant, dramatic salesman. Sensing that Hallam might have more success with Hyman if he were out of the way, B. Clark declared that he would leave immediately for an on-site inspection of the properties, despite the fact that record-breaking snowfalls covered the passes and it was one of the worst winters on record. However, before he departed, the canny professor managed to secure an order for a survey of Ute City from the Surveyor General of the State of Colorado, a document that would allow him to control the development of the townsite.

Then, in February 1880, B. Clark and four companions – Captain Isaac Cooper (who later founded Glenwood Springs), William L. Hopkins (one of Pratt's original partners), Dr. Richardson, and Jack King – set out for Ute City on the long Norwegian skis that the travelers referred to as "snowshoes." Walking atop five to seven feet of snow, they carried on their backs all they needed for the survey, plus letters and newspapers for the news-starved prospectors. It took them nearly four days to travel the seventy miles to Ute City, but by the time they arrived, B. Clark's spirits had not been dampened. He and his party did a line-of-sight survey and presumably inspected Bennett's mining properties, albeit under five feet of snow. Although Gillespie had been gone less than three months, residents apparently agreed when B. Clark changed the name of the camp from Ute City to Aspen. Perhaps the isolated prospectors were pleased to see these signs of progress, especially from someone as entertaining as B. Clark Wheeler.

Seventeen days after it left, the Wheeler party was back in Leadville. Although he had almost certainly done nothing more than ascertain the existence of the mines, B. Clark immediately telegraphed Hyman to inform him that the four principal claims – the Smuggler, the Durant, the Monarch, and the Iron – were more than worth the full purchase price. Hyman was doubtful, but he too must have been a gambler at heart since he decided to try and raise capital to pay the remaining $160,000.

To Hyman's surprise, as soon as he made the investment opportunity public, he was contacted by Abel D. Breed's agent. As a businessman, Hyman knew of Breed's successes in Boulder, but had no idea that he already had investments in the Roaring Fork Valley. Nonetheless, he was pleased when Breed readily agreed to take a one-third interest in the venture. Word of the opportunity spread quickly and the remaining shares sold in a matter of months. Hyman, Hallam, and B. Clark Wheeler were definitely in business.

There remained one small detail: not one of the principals has taken a real look at the properties. So Hyman, who was now back at his Cincinnati headquarters, dispatched a young mining engineer, John B. Farish, to make an on-site inspection. Farish, accompanied by a surveyor and an assayer, left Denver on May 15, 1880. He built what was the area's second log cabin and made a thorough investigation of the properties. He discovered that although the claims looked good, there was a technical glitch. The original owner, Charles Bennett, had hired a surveyor, Jack Christian, to verify and amend his original claims. But soon after he completed work on the Smuggler, Christian was scared off by the rumors of an Indian uprising and fled Ute City before surveying Bennett's other seven claims. Therefore the claims were subject to question and open to conflict with adjacent claims. Hyman demanded a perfect title that would guarantee complete ownership. When Bennett refused to supply perfect titles, Hyman said the deal was off and left Cincinnati for a vacation on Long Island.

Hyman was soon interrupted by an urgent telegram from Hallam, who had arrived in Aspen on May 9 with B. Clark Wheeler and his party. The ore at the Smuggler had finally been assayed, and its rich content made the sale a good one no matter what the status of the other mines. Hallam added that he and Farish had taken great care to cover up their findings in order to avoid a rush to Smuggler Mountain, but secrecy and speed were essential. Hyman took the train west and, on July 1 in Leadville, he signed the papers that made him the primary owner of seven-and-a-half silver mines and two ranches in Aspen, Colorado.

Still, Hyman was plagued by Farish's doubts about the other claims. The only answer seemed to be a personal inspection of the properties. So in mid-July, Hyman and Hallam set off for Buena Vista and the long foot-journey across the Continental Divide to Taylor Pass and down into Aspen via Castle Creek Valley. The trip was a revelation to Hyman. Even though he was not an outdoorsman, the beauty of the environs and the excitement of the mining camp caught his imagination.

In Aspen, the Smuggler Mine was within easy walking distance. In his journal Hyman noted, "I went over to see it many times and wondered to what it would lead."

Hyman made his decision. He decided to keep all but the ranching claims which he sold to the Aspen Town and Land Company. He appointed Charles Hallam, who had recently purchased his own ranch site adjacent to the townsite, as his partner and manager of his mining properties. Henceforth, David Hyman devoted himself to the business end of mining, which he ran from his office in Cincinnati with frequent trips to Denver, New York, and Leadville. He became a skilled financier and an expert on mining law. Hallam, on the other hand, became one of Aspen's most prominent citizens. His wife and family spent summers in Aspen, and throughout the remainder of his life he remained involved in Aspen mining.

Aspen, the Town

Most of the dozen or so prospectors who stayed in Ute City over the winter of 1879–80 huddled together in tents at the future townsite. A few — including Henry Tourtelotte, Warner Root, Henry Staats, and J. Warren Elliott — had wintered in Hunter Creek. They built a cabin in Hunter Creek during the early fall while one of their party members went back to Leadville for more provisions. To the dismay of those who remained, very early and severe snows prevented their companion's return, so supplies were sparse. Occasionally a trip would be made into Ute City, where the Hunter Creek group found that the men of Ute had formed a company to sink a shaft somewhere in the bottom land near the town to see if the bedrock would produce gold. After the shaft reached thirty-five or forty feet, the project had been abandoned.

Root, in speaking of the difficulties of navigating the five-foot snows, mentioned that several Swedes in the camp initiated the prospectors in the craft of making "Norwegian snowshoes." In fact, the snowshoes were crude skis, about twelve feet long, maneuvered with the help of a long pole. Root noted that soon everyone in camp had at least two pair and "it wasn't long before we became experts in the using of them," which made navigation much easier.

In May 1880 B. Clark Wheeler returned with Hallam, J. W. Deane, Byron Shear, Fred C. Johnson, W. W. Williams, and several miners. Deane was an attorney and the official representative of the Aspen Town and Land Company. This company of Philadelphia investors had been formed two months earlier by B. Clark Wheeler on the strength of the survey he made on his first trip to Aspen. The survey gave the Company some legal rights in developing the actual town.

Wheeler and Deane lost no time in laying out the town's first subdivision, Deane's Addition, at the foot of Aspen Mountain. Wheeler then made a finished survey of Aspen's streets, naming them for the Company's officials and pioneers. But in June some of the town's original residents, under the leadership of Colonel George Crittendon, threatened a rebellion against the Aspen Town and Land Company's claim to the townsite. The age-old custom of squatter's rights was supposed to guarantee ownership of the sites they already occupied. Finally, the Company and the residents came to a partial agreement. The Company promised improvements to the town, including roads and a smelter, and the sale of each lot to those currently in possession for a nominal ten dollars. David Hyman's sale of Bennett's two downtown ranchsites to the Company in July added to the strength of the Company's claim, but the confusion about who owned what was never entirely settled. A hundred years later, the county's courts would still be trying to sort out conflicting claims of land, mineral, and water ownership.

Many of the names Wheeler chose for the streets remain today: Hallam, Hyman, Cooper, Deane, Gillespie, Hopkins, etc., but so does the famous "variation." B. Clark intended to lay the streets out running due north and south and due east and west. Apparently he neglected to take into account the variation between magnetic north — as indicated on the compass — and true north. "Ah hell," said Wheeler when confronted with the mistake. "Variation ain't got as far west as this yet." Thus the streets of Aspen are forever askew.

True to its word, during the summer of 1880, the Aspen Town and Land Company cut a road over Taylor and Cottonwood passes to Buena Vista, although Root called it a sorry apology for a road and noted that no smelter was in sight. The population of Aspen swelled to 500 people that summer. The *Leadville Chronicle* described the trip over Independence Pass in its July 11, 1880, issue: "The rapidity of the rise and the uncertainty of the trails are evidenced by the score or more of dead animals which have

Wagons on Independence Pass Road

14

missed their footing and rolled back into the valley. . . . The descent into Independence Gulch surpasses anything the wildest imagination can conjure. The narrow path seems perpendicular, if indeed it does not lean a little backward. Many a burro has ceased from troubling before he reached the bottom. Accommodations can be obtained at Independence, meals 75 cents, oats 25 cents. Leaving Independence, for 20 miles the trail leads across more rocks and swamps than any other 100 miles in the world. . . . A prominent feature is toll bridges. These occur every three or four miles and cost the traveler 25 cents each. Riding that 25 miles is out of the question. It must be walked and the horse led with great care . . . "

The reporter added that there was one secondhand store and four saloons in town, and a log cabin built by William Hopkins, with two doors, one window, and a sod and willow roof. Another account mentioned only twenty tents in the downtown business district. "The Lee House," said Root, " is the only hotel and board costs $10.50 per week." Cooking was done at an open fire in front of the hotel tent, and corn bread and bacon cost twenty-five cents. There was only one wagon in town, and that had been brought into Aspen via sled in pieces and reassembled on arrival.

This midsummer report was outdated almost as soon as it was published. The scores of prospectors who came up through the Eagle Valley or over the mountain passes were soon joined by those who wanted to serve them: merchants, madames, saloonkeepers, millers, builders, blacksmiths, and assayers. Merchant C. H. Jacobs opened for business. James McLaughlin arrived and eventually built Aspen's first hotel, the Clarendon. Delmonico's Restaurant, operated by David Brothers & Winn, opened and served deer, elk, bear, trout, and sheep. Henry Webber & Co. built a store and put in a stock of boots. Brooks & Shaeffer and H. M. Saunders became the first engineers and surveyors to locate in Aspen. Deane, J. Watson, and Byron Shear opened law offices, as did Col. George Crittendon and Joe H. King. Root, the journalist, became a justice of the peace and a constable.

The arrival of four other newcomers probably took place without too much notice, although they were to become instrumental in shaping Aspen's future. Henry P. Cowenhoven, born in Prussia, was a merchant in Indiana. He had joined the Forty-Niners in search of gold but later returned to Indiana. Then, at the age of forty-five, he responded again to the lure of the gold fields in Colorado. He and his wife Margaret and daughter Kate finally settled in Black Hawk, where he had a general store. In 1880, as the prospects there faded, the adventurous Cowenhoven

Kate Cowenhoven Brown

decided to move on. One wonders today what his wife and daughter thought, for Cowenhoven had no particular destination in mind. Perhaps Arizona, he said, or New Mexico. After selling his store, he loaded his stock into two wagons and invited his clerk David Robinson Crockett (D. R. C.) Brown to come along. Brown was only twenty-four and perhaps already involved with Kate. In any case, he agreed, and the four set off, stopping along the way to collect a few debts. They passed through Leadville and continued on to Twin Lakes for outfitting and provisioning. There they met a man named Blodgett who spoke of hostile Indians in the Southwest and suggested that they take a look at the Roaring Fork Valley. So the little party set out for Buena Vista and for the passes beyond.

At this point, the route was little more than a foot track, but the travelers knew that their future lay in the goods loaded in the two wagons, and they were determined to take them along. They reached the summit of Cottonwood Pass in two-and-a-half-days. From there it took them two weeks to cross Taylor Pass and make the steep descent into the Castle Creek Valley, a distance of only ten miles. In the rough spots, the foursome unloaded the wagons, packed the goods on the mules, and Margaret and Kate led the animals around the cliffs, while Brown and Cowenhoven disassembled the wagons and lowered them down the rock faces. Then they reassembled the wagons and began all over again. When they finally reached Ashcroft on July 21, 1880, they saw workmen toiling away on the toll road. In Aspen, Cowenhoven bought a corner lot at Cooper Avenue and Galena Street and began building a house and store.

Cowenhoven and Brown's store was the fourth to open for business. Henry Staats, one of the original 1879 prospectors, wrote that quite a number of the sourdoughs tried to get a look at Kate and get on the right side of 'Grandpap' Cowenhoven by buying supplies, whether they needed them or not. However, as Staats surmised, Brown had the inside track and soon married Kate. In four years the penniless clerk from Nova Scotia would be a millionaire, founding an Aspen dynasty that continues to this day.

Tourtelotte Park, high up Aspen Mt.

Meanwhile, other towns in the area were in the building stages. Henry Tourtelotte built a cabin on his claim high up on Aspen Mountain and began to establish the town he called Tourtelotte Park. Eventually it boasted 300 residents and a tramway that ran between Aspen and Tourtelotte. People could ride in the tramway buckets for $1.25 per round trip.

16

July 4, 1882, Ashcroft

The gold camp of Independence just below Hunter's Pass was founded the summer of 1879 when Billy Belden and a partner found gold on July 4th. They called the mine Independence in honor of the national holiday. The camp and the nearby pass also took on the new name. Most of the camp's claims were soon consolidated under the auspices of the Farwell Consolidated Mining Company of Leadville.

The summer of 1880 also found T. E. Ashcraft busy laying out the townsite of Chloride — sometimes called Castle Forks City — ten miles up Castle Creek. Soon renamed Ashcroft, after the pronunciation of its founder's name, the little city had the advantage of being close to the road over Taylor Pass. Within a year, Ashcroft had a population of over 500 people. The little town of Jackson, renamed Kellogg for its founder, was formed a few miles above Ashcroft, and the town of Highland was located where Castle Creek and Conundrum Creek met.

Real estate speculators from Leadville, including a doctor and a judge, laid out a townsite on the mesa between Castle Creek and Maroon Creek, advertised it widely, and sold several home sites. The developers even succeeded in getting the U.S. Postmaster to locate a post office there. However, only one house was built, the whole scheme collapsed, and the post office building was moved to Aspen.

Although most of Aspen's new citizens left at the first sign of snow, a sturdy core of settlers remained during the winter of 1880–81. This time, in addition to the sourdoughs, there were several married couples and one single woman. Among them were Mr. and Mrs. Cowenhoven, Kate Cowenhoven, David Brown, Mr. and Mrs. Henry Gillespie, and Mr. and Mrs. Warner A. Root. Also present through the winter were B. Clark Wheeler, attorney J. W. Deane, and his partner Byron Shear. They entertained themselves with cultural pursuits organized by Mrs. Gillespie: a literary society, a literary paper, a Sunday school, musicals, and dances. And of course, there was skiing. Warner Root spoke of the Christmas Dinner prepared for the whole camp by the ladies: " . . . a more bountiful feast was never spread amid the wilds of the Rocky Mountains. . . . I am positive that not one of the 300 present, though they live to ripe old age . . . but will pause and say, to the ladies of Aspen can be attributed the pleasantest evening ever spent in Aspen."

By spring of 1881, town began to fill up again. Starting in March, sleighs made regular runs between Twin Lakes and Independence Pass, and from there newcomers walked or rode into town. When they arrived, they found the brand new three-story Clarendon Hotel at the northwest corner of Mill and Durant owned and managed by Mr. and Mrs. James McLaughlin.

In May, 1881, the territory surrounding Aspen, formerly a part of Gunnison County, became Pitkin County—named after Governor Frederick Pitkin. That same month Aspen was incorporated and Aspen's first municipal election took place. There were already 332 voters. Law and order regulations followed soon after and addressed the discharge of firearms, the use of explosives, drunkenness, vagrancy, loitering, confidence games, nudity, graffiti, and other safety and moral issues. The new city fathers would like to have added an extra tax on businesses dealing with liquor and women of ill repute, but they saw them as a necessary part of the single man's entertainment and settled for licensing fees instead.

The next job of the officials was to begin roadbuilding; they started with several roads to the mines on the surrounding mountainsides. Next came the road up Independence Pass, an awesome task that was more a question of leveling than building. Although the first stagecoach crossed the road over the pass in November 1881, advertising "a fine lap robe and heavy wolf robe for every seat," both this and the Taylor Pass toll roads were a source of endless complaint. Potholes and washed-out bridges were the norm and not the exception.

In spite of its isolation, from the beginning Aspen had an air of respectability that was unusual in such a young mining camp. Churches, schools, family homes, and cultural events paralleled the proliferation of businesses and saloons. Hotels, boarding houses, and restaurants also appeared to serve the needs of the single man. The Chloride Restaurant featured trout, venison, and elk steak.

The influx of nearly 800 people created a building boom. Andy McFarlane, a cousin of D. R. C. Brown, had opened a sawmill, first east of town on Ute

Avenue, and later on Castle Creek. Soon it was running fourteen hours a day. Citizens complained that it polluted the stream. Lumber became the town's second largest industry.

There were two more signs of progress: the ladies started a Temperance League, and B. Clark Wheeler started the *Aspen Times* in April 1881. In a strange prophecy of the future, Aspen saw the beginning of the town's craze for culture and sports. After outgrowing temporary quarters in the summer, the Corkhill Opera House opened in December 1881 and became a stop on the touring circuit. The highlight of the season was an extravaganza from the Denver Opera House. The Literary Society still flourished, as did fundraising productions by the Ladies Aid Society. At the other end of the spectrum, the men of Aspen initiated intense baseball contests with teams from Aspen, Ashcroft, and Independence. Horseracing, foot races, cycling races, boxing, and target shooting soon followed. The ice-skating rink became a center for winter social activities, as well as for sport.

While events such as the Grande Soiree Dansante were being held for the gentry in the Clarendon Ballroom, twelve saloons served the hundreds of working men who labored in mining, prospecting, construction, freighting, clerking, and serving. Downtown, tent stores and disreputable vacant lots still flourished among the new wood buildings, but there was a general feeling that Aspen was a place where you could pursue your dream in an orderly environment, mining camp or no mining camp.

In June 1882 the county, with the help of volunteers, managed to string a telegraph wire up to Ashcroft and across Taylor Pass. At last, regular contact with the outside world became a reality.

Mill Street, looking north from the Clarendon Hotel

Aspen, the Mining Community

Although prospecting—or exploration of new mine sites—was still the major interest of Aspen's new population during the summer of 1880, some actual mining did begin. Henry Gillespie and Charles Hallam employed a few miners to sink shafts, drive tunnels, and plan drifts. Even so, work fell more into the category of searching for rich ore than in making an effort to extract ore.

From the beginning, the community recognized Aspen's isolation and its lack of a smelter as major barriers. In 1880 the roads were still incredibly rough. Shipping the ore meant freighting it to Leadville via a mule or jack train. At a cost of eighty dollars a ton—or four cents a pound—only the richest ore made the trip worthwhile. So while several hundred mines were staked out that summer, for the most part mine owners were still betting on the future.

By the summer of 1881 close to a thousand miners made their way over the passes, creating a major building boom in the Roaring Fork Valley but very little in the way of ore shipment. Work on the Smuggler had begun in the spring. By the end of the summer the main shaft reached the eighty-foot level and some ore was shipped by jack train to Leadville. After the miners departed for the winter, as was the custom for this seasonal occupation, Hallam ordered machinery to be freighted over the mountains on the ubiquitous mules. Already, pumps were needed to handle the water that was seeping into the shafts.

But this progress was merely a gesture, and Hallam and every other miner knew it. Aspen needed a smelter that would melt the ore down and extract the silver in a more manageable form. Without a smelter or efficient railway transportation, there was no cost-effective way to get ore out of the Roaring Fork Valley. Talk of a smelter began early and continued for a

Jack train in Aspen

long four years. A Philadelphia corporation began construction of a smelter as early as 1881, but it was never finished. In October 1882 two parties organized the Texas Smelting Company, and through the winter, with the eager help of the townspeople, a building was constructed on a five-acre site on the west side of town. Machinery was transported across the Divide; wood, coke, and charcoal were laid in for the firing. Alas, before the furnace could be blown in, capital ran out and the Texans departed.

A vague loss of optimism pervaded the town. The noisy promoters were losing heart. Farwell shut down operations in Independence and Hallam closed the Smuggler and left with his family for the winter. In the four years since Aspen's founding, although Aspen and Ashcroft had each swelled to 2,000 residents, only a few tons of ore had actually been smelted and not a single bar of silver had been produced. All this was about to be changed by a restless refugee from Macy's Department Store in New York City: Jerome B. Wheeler.

Jerome B. Wheeler Brings New Life to Aspen

Jerome B. Wheeler was born in Troy, New York, in 1841. After the close of the Civil War, where he rose from a private to a colonel, he went into business in Troy, where he made another meteoric rise from bookkeeper to full partner. In 1870 he married Harriet Macy Valentine, the niece of Randolph H. Macy, who founded what became the largest department store in New York. When an unfortunate series of deaths in the family caused a management crisis at Macy's, Wheeler was invited to join as a partner in 1879. He brought excellent business experience to the company, but as an owner of only forty-five percent of the stock he was unable to direct things as he wanted. Therefore, he sought to place his considerable energies and generous salary elsewhere. Among other things, he bought a summer home in Manitou Springs, Colorado. There he met an artist-cum-entrepreneur named Harvey Young. Young, the owner of two Aspen properties (the Morning and the Evening Star at the head of Ophir Gulch), convinced Wheeler that this four-year old town was the perfect place for someone who wanted to make both his fortune and his mark. In November 1882 Wheeler bought the mines from Young for $20,000. In the spring he set forth by stage to take a look at Aspen and his properties.

Jerome B. Wheeler

As a businessman he was quick to see that, indeed, nothing much could be done without a smelter. Three months later his purchase of the half-finished smelter hit the town like a bombshell. Suddenly he was both Aspen's savior and its most prominent citizen. Wheeler took almost a year to put the smelter in shape, but while he was doing so he bought one of Aspen's most valuable mines, the Spar, from the Cincinnati casket-maker Abel D. Breed. Since his original purchase, Breed had been sitting on the investment waiting for the right price. Wheeler paid it and became partners with Henry B. Gillespie. The Galena was part of the same package. The new partners immediately put 50 miners to work.

Meanwhile, Jerome B. proceeded to invest in other areas. He purchased large coal mines thirty miles away in Crested Butte to provide coke and coal for the smelter. He began building a road to the smelter and opened Aspen's first bank: J. B. Wheeler and Company. The bank was capitalized at $100,000. For its permanent headquarters, he bought two lots at the corner of Mill and Cooper and constructed a brick building that opened for business in September 1884. He also hired a highly experienced metallurgist, Walter B. Devereux, to come to Aspen to run the smelter.

The smelter was blown in on July 4, 1884, amidst great celebration and fanfare. That summer 500 miners were at work and production was estimated at $1,260,000 per annum. The smelter reduced ore to a concentrate worth $600 a ton, which was shipped by jack train over Independence Pass to the railhead in Granite and thence to the Pennsylvania Refining Works in Pittsburgh. No one could doubt that Aspen was on its way as a mining town.

1885: Six-Year Old Aspen — Civilized and Sassy

By 1885 Pitkin County had a population of 4,484. Mining, construction, retail merchandising, transportation, and freighting were all booming. There was a brick factory, a planing mill, several sawmills, the smelter, a concentrator, and a sampler. Over 1,000 homes had been built, with more under construction. The Aspen Forwarding Company, owned by Henry Thode and several partners, had a large corral at the east end of Cooper Street with stalls for ninety animals, a blacksmith shop, and plenty of fresh water. Every day the firm's teams moved forty to fifty tons of freight from Aspen to Granite, on the other side of Independence Pass.

The ever-growing population was by now in dire need of a safe supply of drinking water and a water supply that would guard against fire. The previous year, the wooden Clarendon Hotel had burned to the ground. Ever vigilant to an opportunity to make a profit, Cowenhoven and Brown ac-

The Aspen Fire Department

quired water rights to Hunter Creek and Castle Creek and formed the Aspen Water Company. From its waterworks on Castle Creek (now located under the current Castle Creek Bridge and used as a city maintenance building) it piped water two-and-a-half miles into town. When the water was finally turned on, a spontaneous celebration took place with people all over town squirting each other with water from the hoses attached to the new fire hydrants. It worked perfectly.

Soon after, the Aspen Electric Light & Power Company was formed, making Aspen one of the first cities in the state to have entirely electrified streetlights. The electric plant was at the west end of Hallam Avenue across the bridge over Castle Creek. Soon to follow was Aspen's first telephone, located in the office of the Spar Consolidated Mine. It ran from the mine to the home of the company's physician, Dr. B. J. Perry, and an extension ran to Crosby and Reese's Drug Store. The rebuilt Clarendon Hotel was piped for gas, and had three electric lights, an electric alarm, and a call apparatus to reach guests in their rooms.

Street signs and sidewalks were built to complement the growing number of substantial West End homes. Socially, Aspen's elite boasted a lifestyle similar to the wealthy in any other civilized city, complete with gala balls and dances. Young men and women were sent away to school. The families of Gillespie and Henry Webber both had pianos which had been disassembled and freighted over the pass like everything else — on mules. Opera was presented, as was Shakespeare. And travel was a mark of distinction. Hallam Lake, originally used as an ice pond, was made into an amusement park, with boating, fishing, and skating on the lake, and a dance hall on the shore. It even had a tunnel-of-love ride, which came rolling down a ramp off the south ridge of the lake.

But outside of the elite cadre, the vast majority of Aspenites led more middle-class lives, enjoying the perfect weather and the lovely surroundings, along with the rising tide of prosperity. The census counted miners, prospectors, engineers, smelter workers, charcoal burners, sawmill workers, carpenters, contractors, painters, brickmasons, plasterers, butchers, fruit dealers, shoe dealers, teamsters, blacksmiths, doctors, lawyers, druggists, printers, accountants, real estate brokers, school-teachers, hotelkeeper, barbers, cooks, waiters, bartenders, prostitutes, gamblers, and actresses. Lawyers were the most numerous of the professional men. And as in modern times, many working people had more than one job.

J. C. Connor built the first working class subdivision along Deane Street to the foot of Aspen Mountain. The town's consumption of beer was thirty barrels a day in the winter and forty-five barrels a day in the summer. By 1886 there were more than 400 students in Aspen's schools.

Most residents were white, and three out of four were male. There were a few blacks, mulattos, and American Indians, but no Asians. A February 1886 newspaper story recounted the arrival of a young Chinaman who was summarily told by town officials to leave and not to come back. Of the immigrants, the Germans and Irish outnumbered other new Americans, although there were also many from the British Isles and from Canada. The miners from Cornwall in England were called Cousin Jacks. The Germans retained more ethnic identity than the other immigrants, with an active German Social Club, annual dances, and a display of their native costumes. Oklahoma Flats, behind today's Art Museum, was called "Little Sweden."

Many miners were veterans of the Civil War. Thus, there exist many gravestones in Ute Cemetery that indicate only name, date, and regiment. Independence Day was celebrated by the entire town. As it is today, the parade was a highlight followed by contests and entertainment. Much of the activity took place at the race track located in the west end of town. There, in the grandstands, a crowd of 500 people watched drilling matches among teams and individuals. Then came a group of riders, dressed as knights, competing in tilts and tournaments. Horse races brought an end to a perfect day. This festive display of nineteenth century Americana had evolved in only six years; tiny Ute City with its ragged cluster of tents had become a prosperous little city on the brink of greatness.

Parade through town

1887: The Railroad Arrives

No incident in Aspen's history changed the town more quickly than the arrival of the railroad. Until 1887, Aspen, always a slave to its geographic isolation, still struggled to ship its goods into and out of town. Then, in a period of just a few months, Aspen had not one, but two railroads.

The Denver and Rio Grande Railroad was the brainchild of William Jackson Palmer, who dreamed of a railroad that would run north to south for the length of the Rockies. The political and legal complications surrounding this concept finally convinced Palmer to look to a more western route and take advantage of the boom in the mining camps. By 1880 his "Baby Road," so named for the small size of the corporation and its narrow gauge, had reached Leadville. Palmer pressed on towards Salt Lake, sending branches into likely silver camps. Although the railroad reached nearby Crested Butte, talk of extending it into Aspen came to nothing until 1886. Then, bolstered by new leadership and money, the D. & R. G., already at Red Cliff, began building towards Glenwood Springs where it would eventually turn southeast up the valley to Aspen.

Meanwhile, Jerome B. Wheeler and James J. Hagerman, with financial assistance from D. R. C. Brown and E. T. Butler, had taken control of the Colorado Midland Railroad Company. In early 1886 they brought a standard gauge line into Leadville with the intention of continuing into Aspen. The race was on.

The Midland chose to take the route west from Leadville across the Continental Divide, through a tunnel to be named for Hagerman, then down the Frying Pan River to Basalt, and then up the Roaring Fork River to Aspen. Once there, it would enter Aspen on the south side along West Aspen Mountain, with a depot on Deane Street at the base of Aspen Mountain. Unfortunately, that route required the Midland to build bridges over both Castle Creek and Maroon Creek, while the D. & R. G. simply had to run along the north side of the Roaring Fork. Although the Midland reached Maroon Creek as early as September, there it stayed waiting for materials to bridge the river's torrents. Meanwhile, the D. & R. G. forged ahead, with its first work train reaching the Aspen depot on North Mill Street on October 27, 1887. The first official train with its twenty-five cars came in on November 1 at 8:22 p.m.

Aspen had never seen such a celebration. There were speeches from dignitaries such as Governor Adams and Senator Teller, bonfires, fireworks, a parade of carriages and horsemen, and, of course, the grand arrival of twenty-five cars along with the stirring sound of the locomotive's whistles. The exuberant crowd led the D. & R. G. officials, celebrities, and excursionists towards the Clarendon Hotel through a town ablaze with decorations, welcome signs, and Chinese lanterns. A huge banquet was then held at the Corkhill Opera House, where the feast included green turtle soup, oysters, and buffalo tongue. Meanwhile, a giant barbecue was held for 600 of the railroad construction workers. It is said that everyone in town stayed up all night, even the children.

On February 4, 1888, the Midland arrived, and before long Aspen was crisscrossed with feeder lines to all of the major mines. The arrival of the two railroads triggered an economic transformation, moving Aspen from small town to a busy industrial hub almost instantaneously.

The Colorado Midland on the Maroon Creek Trestle

Aspen's Silver Heyday

Until 1887 Aspen had been a collection of thousands of claims. Perhaps only a few hundred of those were actually worked, and only a small percentage of those produced and made a profit. But following the arrival of the railroad, the larger owners began to buy up the smaller working claims. The odds on making money from a silver mine were long, and larger owners were better able to withstand the expenses.

The business of getting silver out of the resistant mountains was not only labor intensive, but was also rife with litigation. The huge Apex suit involving the Durant, the Emma, and the Aspen mines had been settled only after three years of bitter combat in the courts of Aspen and Denver. The quarrel centered around the concept of the apex—a vein of ore that is exposed on the surface. According to mining law, the original claimant had to locate the boundaries of his claim in such a way as to include the top of the exposed vein. If the vein was continuous, the owner had the right to follow the vein underground, an activity that would certainly take him into the underground space of surrounding surface claims. The claims without a lode of their own, but located along the sides of the apex claim, were called sideline claims. David Hyman and his associates were the owners of the Durant and the Spar, claims that covered the apex vein where it surfaced on Aspen Mountain. Several other mines, including the Aspen, the Little Giant, and the Emma, were sideline claims.

In 1884 the Aspen was leased from its owners by J. D. Hooper, Aspen's mayor, and by Charles Todd. In November, after several months of discouraging work and only sixty days before their lease was up, they struck a rich vein of ore. They worked feverishly, stockpiling their ore in a vacant lot downtown. A fascinating aside to this story involves the original owners Elmer Butler, Louis Stone, and Daniel Dunsmore. Previous to the lease to Hooper, Stone traded his one-third ownership of the Aspen to D. R. C. Brown to settle a debt of $250. Dunsmore sold his interest to J. B. Wheeler for $5,000, and Butler tried to sell his share for $100 but found no takers. As a result of this casual transaction, Brown and Butler made their fortunes, and Wheeler greatly increased his.

However, following Hooper's strike, David Hyman, although he had no capital to start work on the Durant, realized that if he were to gain all he was entitled to according to the apex law of 1872, he would have to take the owners of the Aspen to court. The whole town took sides while the case was tried in Pitkin County's District Court. Nearly everyone favored the sideliners, but Judge Goddard found the law clear and ruled in favor of Hyman and the apexers. The decision was appealed and the case was

Bertha Kelley and a friend in front of the Mollie Gibson Mine

moved to federal court in Denver. Again the judge ruled in favor of
Hyman. By now, after two years of litigation, Hyman's financial resources
were at an end and the bitterness of the opponents made compromise appear impossible. However, through the auspices of Midland president
James Hagerman, who also had interest in mines that sidelined the Durant,
an agreement was reached. Hyman, Wheeler, Butler, and Cowenhoven put
all of their shares together in a company aptly called the Compromise Mining Company. As fate would have it, the Aspen Mine produced silver worth
$11 million in the next five years while the Durant produced very little.
Thus, Hyman made his first fortune, almost all of it from work his competitors had started.

From 1887 to late 1892, shipments of ore increased from 1,500 to 4,000
tons a week. Rather than reflecting more producing mines, this was due
primarily to increased productivity in eight bonanza mines: the Aspen, the
Compromise, the Smuggler, the Argentum-Juanita, the Park Regent, the
consolidated Aspen Mining and Smelting Company, and the Mollie Gibson Consolidated Mining Company, which eventually included the Mollie
Gibson, the Lone Pine, the Silver King, and the Sargent.

The Smuggler, still owned by Hyman and Hallam, did not truly become a
bonanza until 1890, when rich ore bodies were discovered on the surface.
Its neighbor, the Mollie Gibson, was also a late bloomer. First claimed in
1880 and then acquired by Henry Gillespie and Byron Shear, it revealed a
fabulous streak of ore that assayed out with 5,000 ounces per ton in 1889.
The Mollie Gibson became one of the richest mines in the history of
American silver mining. The publicity surrounding the Mollie made Aspen

internationally famous, and its owners reaped great rewards. But the most spectacular winner in the story was Byron Shear, who came to Aspen without a penny in 1880, went to work for B. Clark Wheeler for $2.50 a day plus board, and now headed to Washington D.C. to build a huge mansion.

Meanwhile, Aspen's millionaires were building their own mansions on Bullion Row, as Hallam Street was known. Downtown was punctuated with numerous all-brick blocks, many of them built and owned by a single individual. Cowenhoven, Brown, Wheeler, and Hyman all had their own blocks. A horse-drawn streetcar traversed one end of downtown to the other. One hundred and fifty people had telephones of their own. Jerome B. Wheeler's Hotel Jerome and Wheeler Opera House had opened in 1889 to much fanfare and a feeling of rare satisfaction to the citizenry. At last Aspen had its own brick hotel and a suitable location for cultural events. Other buildings included the dignified brick courthouse, still in use today, the Armory, now Aspen's City Hall, and, of course, Wheeler's impressive three-story brick bank.

1893: the End of an Era

Fourteen years after the first brave explorers made their way down from Independence Pass into a deserted valley, Aspen had a population of 10,000, making it the third largest town in Colorado. Aspen had become a little industrial enclave. Samplers, smelters, reduction works, concentrators, and trains spewed dirt and smoke. Machinery, now powered by electricity, throbbed from every mine. The hillsides were growing bare from the use of lumber for fuel and building. The streams were polluted and the noise was constant. Tramways reached far up the mountains, much like today's lift towers, carrying thousands of tons of ore down to the ore building and the railroad sidings below. A huge nugget of high-grade silver was yet to be taken out of the Smuggler Mine. It would weigh nearly a ton and would have to be broken into three pieces to hoist it out of the mine. There were numerous ore-processing plants in town, including the Holden Mining and Smelting Works — often called the Lixiviation Works — which is now a museum on the Marolt Property, west of Aspen.

More than 3,000 men were employed in mining operations, most of them for a daily wage of three dollars. The change in shifts saw a fascinating stream of men meandering up the mountain with lunchboxes and lights, merging into lines like so many ants, and finally entering the individual mines. Three times a day, at 8 a.m., 4 p.m., and midnight, there was a cacophony of sound — a different whistle from each mine — as the miners changed shifts. The work, hundreds of feet below the earth's surface, was difficult and dangerous. But, like the Aspenites of today, they may have found the excitement and the beauty of the environment reward enough. Family homes were available for twenty-five dollars a month. There were good schools, a hospital that the miners helped build by contributing a day's pay, theatrical productions, boxing matches, professional baseball teams, wonderful picnic sites, the annual Miners' Union Ball, many social opportunities, and always the hope of striking it rich. The future looked bright for almost all of Aspen's citizens. All that changed with incredible rapidity.

In the spring of 1893 the failing economy in the rest of the United States began to take its toll. Depression began making its way to the Rockies and finally into the mining camps. In 1890 the Sherman Silver Purchase Act nearly doubled silver purchases, but it also radically increased the amount of money in circulation. President Grover Cleveland believed that it was this act that threatened to undermine the Treasury's gold reserves. In 1893 he called a special session of congress to repeal the Sherman Act and demonetize silver. As word reached Colorado, silver prices began to fall. Within months 30,000 silver miners in Colorado were out of work. The Sherman Act was officially repealed on November 4, 1893. By the end of 1893, eighty percent of Aspen's enterprises were bankrupt. Thousands of suddenly destitute Aspenites and their families moved on and most of Aspen's mines closed their doors forever. ●

Aspen as seen from Aspen Mountain in about 1893

The Quiet Years: 1894–1935

For a city that was only fourteen years old, Aspen, then as now, was remarkably resilient. From 1883 to 1893 its population had grown from 1,000 people to 10,000, with perhaps another 5,000 people in the county. And although the crash of silver sparked the departure of thousands of recently destitute merchants and miners, when all was said and done the population of the "Crystal City of the Rockies" remained at 8,500 for the next four years. It was not until the end of the century that it went below 5,000.

Those who left — permanently affected by mining fever — went on to other camps, primarily Cripple Creek, where it was said that every other merchant was from Aspen. Those who stayed eked out a living as best as was possible.

After The Fall

By the spring of 1894 some of the mines had reopened. The Smuggler, the Mollie Gibson, the Aspen, and the Cowenhoven Tunnel together employed 350 men at a reduced wage. Perhaps another 700 miners managed to scratch out a living by leasing mines from the owners. They sold their ore for a pittance: 59 cents an ounce, down from 87 cents in 1892, and $1.10 in 1887.

Some of the recently unemployed went into commerce. Aspen had two railroads, several lumbermills, a brewery, a foundry, schools, power companies, various commercial establishments, civic projects, hotels, and restaurants. Although spending money grew increasingly scarce, many businesses continued to function and offer employment.

Some hard-rock men turned to the soil to make a living. Ranching and farming had been an important part of the Roaring Fork Valley economy since the 1880s. Attracted by the prospect of cheap land and beautiful country, farmers and ranchers arrived soon after the prospectors, creating the valley's first non-transient population. Many of the ranching families originated from the region near Aosta in northern Italy, on the south side of Mount Blanc. Many of their names can still be found in the Roaring Fork Valley phone book: Arbaney, Cerise, Gerbaz, Trentaz, and Vagneur. And although agricultural interests tended to be centered downvalley, much of the land that lay in between the rocky slopes of Aspen was used for crops or livestock.

Horse-drawn sleighs loading produce

In 1884 a road between Glenwood and Aspen was completed, creating a byway for those who worked the land, as well as for those who mined it, and Aspen quickly became a supply center. Farming and ranching communities included Woody Creek, Capitol Creek, Brush Creek, Owl Creek, Watson, Sopris Creek, El Jebel, and Carbondale. Farmers found that crops such as oats, hay, buckwheat, spring wheat, potatoes, and onions, irrigated by ditches that ran from the rivers to the fields, grew well even at 7,000–8,000 feet above sea level.

Coal was discovered near Carbondale and Redstone and provided viable employment until 1908, when the decline of mining and smelting throughout Colorado affected the need for coal fuel.

A tiny tourist industry continued to thrive during the summer, when fly-fishermen came to test the Roaring Fork and Frying Pan rivers, the latter so named for the fish that leapt straight from the river into the pan.

Meanwhile, after the first chaotic months following demonetization, life in Aspen went on much as it had before. Those who couldn't make it had left, much as they had arrived, with little more than the clothes on their backs. Those who remained continued to lead the orderly life that had always set Aspen apart from the raucous camps of Leadville and Central City. Children went to school. Ladies attended their social clubs. Single men went to the saloons. Sporting events retained their great popularity. Entertainments were presented at the Wheeler Opera House. And the newspapers continued to publish, optimistically predicting the return of the silver standard and Aspen's return to the prosperity of 1892.

This, however, was not to be.

The Slow Slide Downward

In spite of the best efforts of the mining lobbies, mining stocks fell steadily after 1894. The mineral output of Pitkin County fell from four million dollars in 1894 to less than a million in ten years. The population fell proportionately from 8,500 in 1894, to 3,303 in 1900, and to 1,834 in 1910.

Only one major mining venture was attempted during this era – D. R. C. Brown's Free Silver Mining Company. The project, started in 1894, was an attempt to drive a shaft that would intersect the rich ores of the Smuggler and the Mollie Gibson at a depth of 1,500 feet. By 1897 the shaft was completed. Sure enough, the silver was there; unfortunately, water was there too, flooding in from all of the tunnels dug beneath the surface of Smuggler Mountain for the past nineteen years. Believing that electric power was the answer, the investors convinced Brown to install new generators at his Castle Creek plant to power the mine's pumps. And indeed, the huge pumps removed all but the last sixty-five feet of water at the eleventh level. In 1910 the owners tried a radical experiment: bringing in deep-sea divers from New York to clear the obstructions underwater and get the pumps operating. They succeeded, and Smuggler Mountain released another $2,000,000 worth of ore in the next year. But even that was not enough to justify the costs. In 1911 the owners of the Smuggler, the Mollie Gibson, and the Free Silver announced that they had reached their financial limits and would shut down. In 1919 the pumps were finally pulled from the Smuggler, allowing the inexorable flooding from the scores of shafts that had ventured deeper and deeper in search of silver.

Mining elsewhere in Aspen did continue, but in a more and more limited way. Over the next twenty years low grade ores of lead, zinc, and silver continued to provide a living for leaseholders on Smuggler Mountain, Aspen Mountain, Ashcroft, and the back of Aspen Mountain. A few mines, in-

cluding the Midnight Mine, owned by the Willoughby brothers, the Henry Clay, the Smuggler, and the Durant leased by the Herron brothers, and Billy Tagert's Montezuma Mine, continued production of minerals into the forties. Work at the Smuggler, which is still owned by David Hyman's descendants, continues to this day.

Divers in the Smuggler Mine in 1910

33

The Fate of Aspen's Most Famous Pioneers

Henry B. Gillespie, the first entrepreneur to sniff out the possibilities of Aspen, briefly promoted other mining camps in Aspen and then retired to his luxurious ranch twenty-four miles west of Aspen, where El Jebel is now located. Gillespie, however, was not one to stay inactive. In 1902 he departed for Dutch Guinea where he hoped to make a fortune of another kind. There he contracted malaria and died after a brief illness in 1902.

B. Clark Wheeler, the flamboyant huckster who arrived in Aspen on snowshoes, bought the local newspaper, the *Aspen Times*, and enjoyed a colorful career as a journalist, a mining investor, and Aspen's mayor. But his resources were not enough to keep him in Aspen after the crash of 1893. In the end, the strike that provided for his comfortable old age in California came from the silver mines of Sonora, Mexico.

Jerome B. Wheeler, Aspen's one-time savior, was a victim of overoptimism and overinvestment. His Aspen bank had been among the first victims of the demise of silver, and soon thereafter Wheeler moved to Colorado Springs. There, among the other mining entrepreneurs, he lived in comfort, insisting that his 1901 bankruptcy was merely a temporary setback. That was not the case, and he died in 1918 without regaining his fortune.

Henry P. Cowenhoven, affectionately known as "Pap," died in Aspen in 1896. This adventurous merchant, who brought a wagonload of trading goods over Taylor Pass a year after silver was discovered in Aspen, had made millions through his mining and commercial enterprises. His daughter Kate had married his clerk, D. R. C. Brown, whose fortunes surpassed even those of his father-in-law.

Brown, although he traveled frequently with his family, did not desert Aspen when lean times came. He had long since diversified his interests, owning miles of real estate along with the water and electric companies, and acres of mines. From a penniless clerk, he became Aspen's most prominent homegrown millionaire. When he died in 1930, townspeople formed an honor guard that accompanied him to the top of Independence Pass. His son, D. R. C. Brown, Jr., was an original investor in the Aspen Skiing Corporation and eventually became its president. His grandchildren and great grandchildren continue to be involved in Aspen to this day.

David M. Hyman had never been an Aspen resident, but he continued his mining interests there, even after the silver crisis. Although the Mollie Gibson was essentially played out, Hyman was instrumental in reopening the Smuggler, the Durant, and the Aspen, helping to keep the mining industry alive and functioning.

1910 to 1935: Life Goes On

Those who managed to remain in Aspen through the "quiet years" remember that period with great fondness. Although the population shrank to a low of 700 people in 1930, and, generally speaking, survival was a struggle, the residents simply liked living there. Even though money was short, beauty and tranquillity were not. Aspen Mountain bloomed with chokecherries and flowers, and slowly greened over the scars of the mines.

Store interior

There was a good hospital, a doctor, a dentist, two churches, a decent legal system, plenty of power, a movie theatre, ample merchants to supply all the necessaries, the Hotel Jerome soda fountain, a dairy, a mortician, and several groceries. The schools were considered good. Automobile travelers could come and go, either on the newly two-laned Aspen/Glenwood road or over Independence Pass. And although the Colorado Midland stopped operations in 1918, the Denver & Rio Grande Railroad maintained rail service until well after the ski boom. Mayor Charles Wagner, formerly a tailor, managed to keep the city operating on almost nothing ($4,400 in 1925).

Hyman Avenue and Galena

Isis Theatre

Although he served as both mayor and marshal for almost two decades, he is chiefly remembered for having kept the water ditches free of debris. Unlike today's Aspen, politics were such a non-issue, that there was no city election from 1936 to 1947.

While the Wheeler Opera House burned down in 1912 — most agree by the hand of the owner, since it caught fire twice within two weeks — entertainment came to Aspen in 1913 in the form of talkies at the Dreamland Theater (which used the seats from the gutted Wheeler), and later at the Isis. Saturday night concerts were also held at the Jerome. Once, Barnum and Bailey pitched their circus tents where Aspen Meadows now stands.

Aspen was a haven for social clubs, annual dances, and celebrations. There was a parade and horse racing on the Fourth of July. Families hiked, camped, and rode horses in the uncrowded mountains. Children swam in the Roaring Fork or in Sullivan's Pond. In the winter, young people sledded down Monarch Street, skied down the hills near the present high school, ice-skated at the free rink on Galena and Hopkins, and roller-skated in the Armory.

The town prided itself on being hard working, honest, sincere, and self-reliant. Said one native, "It was the most heavenly spot on earth."

The Beginning of the Ski Era: 1936–1950

Strangely enough, Aspen's rebirth began in another picturesque alpine village. Garmisch-Partenkirchen, in the heart of the German Alps, was the host to the 1936 Winter Olympics. There Theodore Ryan, a wealthy easterner, met America's bobsled champion William Fiske III. Both were enthusiastic outdoorsmen with a special love for skiing. Bemoaning the dearth of really first-class ski resorts in the United States, they agreed to keep in touch just in case one of them spotted a good development opportunity.

The next chapter in the saga took place the following summer in Palo Alto, California. Thomas J. Flynn, an Aspenite who arrived in Aspen as a six-year old with his father in a buckboard in 1887, met Fiske at a party in Pasadena. Over cocktails, Flynn regaled Fiske with tales of Aspen and its multiple opportunities. Flynn was hoping to unload a few of his mining properties on Aspen Mountain, but what interested the young Pasadena businessman was not the mines in the snapshot Flynn showed him, but the geography. The long, snowy sweep of Little Annie Basin, with its wonderful reaches of untouched powder, struck a resounding chord. Flynn, nothing if not flexible, was glad to elaborate on the fabulous downhill slopes encompassing his own mountain real estate.

A month later the two men were in Aspen. Flynn had already spread the word to the town stalwarts such as Midnight Mine owners Fred and Frank Willoughby, Montezuma Mine owner Billy Tagert, Smuggler operator John Herron, Hotel Jerome owner Laurence Elisha, shoemaker Mike Magnifico, merchant Francis Kalmes, and mayor Mike Garrish. The inheritors of Aspen's craze for sports of all kinds, these men and their fellow citizens were perfectly willing to believe that Aspen's future could lie not in silver, but in snow. Already they knew the enchantment of Aspen's brilliant sun against the sparkling drifts of snow. They also loved the winter traditions of sleigh rides, sledding, and skating. In Aspen, unlike in the city, the outdoors was used as much in the long winter as it was in the summer. Many Aspenites had either tried skiing or seen others glide gracefully down the winter slopes. Some had childhood memories of the miners making their way down Little Annie or Aspen Mountain balancing the twelve-foot "Norwegian snowshoes" with a twenty-foot pole. Long before the turn of the century, Aspenites held ski races in which they waxed their wooden slats for maximum speed and sped up to seventy mph down the mountain.

In any case, the Willoughbys readily agreed to give the the California investor a grand tour of Aspen Mountain's potential ski slopes. They met Fiske and Flynn in August 1936 at the head of Queen's Gulch off Castle Creek Road. From there they drove up the Midnight Mine Road, finally reaching the top. The astonished Fiske was greeted by brilliant sunshine and the long, open slope of Little Annie Basin. Opposite him were the towering spires of Hayden, Maroon, Pyramid, Castle, and Cathedral peaks, still snow-covered in the midst of summer. This stunning sight convinced Fiske that in this magnificent valley lay his future.

Aspen's First Ski Lodge

Fiske lost no time in making his move. He took an option on land near the old townsite of Highland, by the junction of Castle Creek and Conundrum Creek, and called Ted Ryan to tell him that he had found their winter playground. Fiske left Aspen in a few days, but soon returned with Ryan, Los Angeles realtor Robert Rowan, and several other investors. By the fall of 1936 they had formed the Highland-Bavarian Corporation, bought the land at the base of Hayden and 300 acres of Billy Tagert's placer claim near the old ghost town of Ashcroft, and started construction on the sixteen-bed lodge that was to house the area's first ski tourists. They had also retained Italian skier and mountaineer, Gunther Lange, and Swiss mountaineer and engineer Andre Roch, to survey the Roaring Fork and Castle Creek valleys in order to get recommendations for the ideal location of downhill ski runs. The two Europeans arrived just in time to begin their work before the snow fell. Many of the local men knew the mountains like the back of their hands; they guided Lange and Roch up the rocky gullies and across the high meadows of Aspen Mountain and nearby Mount Hayden.

Roch and friends at the Highland Bavarian, 1936

Meanwhile, work on the Highland-Bavarian Lodge continued at an unprecedented pace with twenty carpenters and stone masons from Glenwood Springs. Just four-and-a-half months after Billy Fiske had his first glimpse of the Roaring Fork Valley, the lodge was finished. The accommodations were rough, but ready; the lodge keeper provided the bunks, but the guests brought their own sleeping bags. Opening day was December 26, 1936. The lodge's first paying guests were Denverites William V. Hodges, Jr., his brother Joseph, Martha Wilcox, Polly Grimes, Frank Ashley, and Gretl Arndt. The crusty old sourdough Billy Tagert, who owned the Montezuma Mine above Ashcroft, carried the skiers in a four-horse sleigh up to the top of Little Annie Basin for the long run down through unpacked powder snow. For more variety, the sportsmen and women embarked on

First ski ascent of Mt. Hayden by Andre Roch and Los Alamos Ranch Ski Team, March, 1937

an arduous climb up the lower slopes of Mount Hayden to enjoy what must have been a thrilling and very challenging run down into the Castle Creek Valley. A few of them even bushwhacked up over Richmond Hill above the Midnight Mine and skied through Tourtelotte Park and down the face of Aspen Mountain for a warm drink at the Hotel Jerome. Roch, Lange, Fiske, Ryan, Rowan, and their guests now possessed an essential piece of knowledge: this was the deepest, lightest powder they had ever known.

Meanwhile, Roch taught the locals how to ski. Fred Willoughby proved to be a fast learner. He won Aspen's first official race: the Aspen Alpine Senior Trophy race of 1937. He and twenty other new skiing enthusiasts formed the Roaring Fork Winter Sports Club, with his brother Frank as the first president.

Roch and Lange departed for Europe in the spring of 1937, just eight months after their arrival. They left behind a complete blueprint of their plan for Highland-Bavarian's winter sports center. The north-facing slopes of Mount Hayden, they decided, were by far the most suitable for an extensive network of downhill runs. They suggested that an aerial tram be built from Ashcroft to the summit of Mount Hayden. On Aspen Mountain, because of its proximity to Aspen's tiny commercial center, they recommended a long downhill run, which they mapped out in detail for clearing when summer arrived.

Highland-Bavarian's principals quickly applied for a special use permit from the U. S. Forest Service to begin surveying for lifts and trails. Eager to promote skiing in Colorado, the state legislature approved a bond issue for $650,000 towards the construction of the aerial tramway and an Ashcroft hotel. The Highland-Bavarian Corporation purchased the land that is now Ashcroft, and Tom Flynn began the task of raising more money for the project. Among those who invested were Denverites Joseph Hodges, William Hodges, Jr., Frank Ashley, and George Berger.

The resort was in its infancy, but already the word was spreading of some of the most exciting skiing this side of the European Alps. Otto Schneibs, the "Father of American Skiing," had brought his Dartmouth Sports Club out for a look via a ski train in February; a little core of Denver skiers were making frequent trips to Aspen; and Lange and Roch raved about their new find to the skiers of Europe.

Skiing Aspen Mountain

In July 1937, unwilling to waste any time, the Roaring Fork Winter Sports Club and crews from Roosevelt's Works Projects Administration (WPA) used the short summer months to clear Aspen's first ski run exactly as designed by Andre Roch. Roch Run was three-and-a-half miles long and dropped 2,000 vertical feet. It started at the top of today's lift #8 terminal and followed the ridge down Zaugg Park, through little Corkscrew, then east of Ruthie's Run, through Corkscrew, and finished at the upper end of Monarch Street. Racers reached the start by climbing up Corkscrew or by riding in trucks to the Midnight Mine on the back side of the mountain. From there they were hauled to the top by a snow tractor. It was said to be the steepest run in America.

The first lift, the now-famous boat tow, was also constructed that summer. It was located just to the west of the new ski trail and consisted of two sleds (or boats) capable of carrying ten passengers each. An old Model A Ford

Riding the boat tow lift

engine, donated by Jerome owner Laurence Elisha, powered the tow, which was hooked up to half-inch cable and two old mine hoists that the Willoughbys brought from the Midnight Mine. Using a jig-back system, it ran up to the bottom of the present day Corkscrew, allowing skiers either to take the short run down or hike up the other half of Roch Run. Passengers paid ten cents per ride and felt it was worth every penny. Parts of the old boat tow can still be seen at the top of Aspen Street near lift 1A.

By 1938 the Roaring Fork Winter Sports Club, renamed the Aspen Ski Club, was ready to host its first ski race: the Western Amateur Championship. Aspen's residents began to see that this wild fad called skiing might just be what the sleepy little town had been waiting for. In the summer and fall of 1938 the Ski Club, with the help of the WPA, moved forward with three more projects. A forty-meter jump, named for the Willoughbys, was built at the foot of Aspen Mountain over the old Veteran Mine to encourage more nordic ski competitions. A warming hut was built at the top of Roch Run and a Ski Club house was built at the top of Monarch Street.

Roch Run as seen from Mill Street

Meanwhile, word of Aspen Mountain's exciting terrain was spreading rapidly to skiers throughout the nation. One early visitor was broadcaster Lowell Thomas. Returning from a visit to Averill Harriman's new ski resort, Sun Valley, he suggested to his companions that they stop in Aspen. There, Laurence Elisha of the Hotel Jerome assigned his young son Don to guide the visitors up Queen's Gulch to the Midnight Mine, over Richmond Hill, and down the face of the mountain. Like today's Aspen youngsters, Don must have been a very competent skier. On the way up, remembers Thomas, they rousted Mike Magnifico out of his mountain cabin and commandeered the willing Frank Willoughby at the mine for a glorious afternoon of skiing. Thomas became one of Aspen's most enthusiastic supporters, annually broadcasting his popular program from the Hotel Jerome.

Lowell Thomas

Another 1939 visitor was Elizabeth Paepcke. Young Mrs. Paepcke, the wife of industrialist Walter Paepcke, had two house guests from Washington D.C. at their ranch in Larkspur, Colorado. Both had

41

brought their skis, so when the pipes froze, she decided to distract her friends with a ski trip to Aspen. They stayed at the Jerome; the price was right — three dollars a night — but the food, said Mrs. Paepcke later, was awful. Animal heads decorated the lobby walls, and guests could relax in the big wicker rockers that faced the uninterrupted view of the mountain. Mrs. Paepcke added that there were plenty of spittoons and old timers who knew how to use them. Their skill was demonstrated one evening when a sourdough spit accurately across Mrs. Paepcke's lap into the spittoon on the other side of her rocker.

To reach the ski slope, the next morning the party made its way up the back of Aspen Mountain in a truck shared with miners working the Midnight Mine. While Mrs. Paepcke's guests — expert skiers — tested their skill with an exhilarating run down the face of Aspen Mountain, the inexpert Elizabeth snowplowed down the road. But her enthusiasm was undampened. Mrs. Paepcke was enchanted with Aspen, and on her return to Chicago, she raved about it to her husband Walter. He was not to make his first visit to Aspen until 1945, but when he did he made an indelible mark.

Ski Racing Takes Off

In 1939 the Aspen Ski Club hosted its first sanctioned ski race: the Southern Rocky Mountain Ski Association Downhill and Slalom Championships. The only lift was still the boat tow, now being operated by D. R. C. Brown, Jr.'s, brother Fletcher. Mike Magnifico turned his shoe shop into a ski shop, Aspen's first.

In 1941 the National Alpine Championships brought the nation's best racers to Aspen. The top finishers were Toni Matt and Dick Durrance. Matt, a famous Austrian racer, called Roch Run the best downhill course he had ever skied. Durrance began a lifelong love affair with Aspen. Other racers who clocked good times were Aspen native D. R. C. Brown, Jr., who would become president of the Aspen Skiing Corporation; Bill Janss, who

The 1941 Nationals

would be the primary developer of Snowmass Village; and longtime Aspen sportsman Barney McLean. A young architect, Fritz Benedict, who would later be an important figure in Aspen's postwar development, came to race but declared himself "outclassed." Already, with only one run and a very primitive lift,

Aspen was becoming a mecca for serious skiers.

Meanwhile, on the Castle Creek side of the mountain, Fiske, Flynn, and Ryan continued to work on their project at Mount Hayden. Ryan hired a New York architect, Elley Husted, to study the Ashcroft area. Husted thought that a community similar to Williamsburg would be more appropriate than Ryan's concept of a little Swiss village. Oddly enough, Ashcroft's last resident, miner Jack Leahy who had died the previous year, had suggested the same thing in 1911. He saw Ashcroft as the Switzerland of Colorado complete with cuckoo clocks and yodeling Tyroleans, thus giving tourists the opportunity to see the country of hardy mountaineers without ever crossing the Atlantic.

It seemed that Aspen was finally on its way. But the war in Europe began to make itself felt even in distant Colorado. When Pearl Harbor was bombed in December 1941, and the United States declared war against the Axis, the Highland-Bavarian project was put on hold indefinitely. Billy Fiske joined the RAF as a pilot and in only a few short months became a national statistic: the first American pilot in the RAF to lose his life. Ted Ryan joined the Army and Flynn turned his interests elsewhere. Throughout America leisure pursuits such as skiing took a back seat to the war for the next four years.

The 10th Mountain Division

Before he left Aspen, Ted Ryan, ever the visionary, contacted the Army's 87th Mountain Infantry Regiment (soon to become the 10th Mountain Division) and offered to lease Ashcroft and the lodge to its troops for training purposes for just one dollar a year. Although the Army ultimately chose Camp Hale near Leadville as a training headquarters, a detachment stayed in Ashcroft while Camp Hale was being built. Later, Aspen became a leave center for the troops of the 10th Mountain Division.

The ski troops loved Aspen. They didn't mind traveling the eighty-two miles from Camp Hale over Battle Mountain to the Roaring Fork Valley, if it meant a weekend pass where you could party and ski. And Aspen had all the charm, panache, and excitement that the much nearer Leadville lacked. When the troops arrived, they slept wherever they could. If the Hotel Jerome was full, they bivouacked on the floor. After a long day of hiking and skiing down the mountain, the 10th mountaineers made straight for the Jerome Bar for a refreshing and lethal drink called the Aspen Crud — a tall, thick milk shake from the Jerome Ice Cream Parlor spiked with ninety proof bourbon.

Tenth Mountain Division troops marching down Main Street in Aspen

When the troops weren't skiing or drinking, they were looking around. Many of them liked what they saw. The setting was idyllic, the skiing was glorious, and a miner's cabin could be purchased for a song. A number of them resolved to return to Aspen after the war, and many of them did — Friedl Pfeifer, Fritz Benedict, Bil Dunaway, Stuart Mace, Dick Wright, Johnny Litchfield, Steve Knowlton, Shady Lane, Bert Bidwell, Bob Lewis, Percy Rideout, Harry Poschman, and Aspen native George Tahcowchek.

Pfeifer was Austrian born and joined the 10th Mountain Division directly from his position as ski school director in Sun Valley. Hiking into Aspen during one of the division's summer maneuvers, he looked from Red Mountain across to Aspen Mountain and was strongly reminded of the terrain in St. Anton, one of Austria's great ski areas. From then on, he spent every spare moment exploring the face of Aspen Mountain, envisioning dozens of ski trails rushing down the steep faces to meet the town. He even went so far as to speak to the city council. "I am coming back after the war," he said, "and this town is going to be my home. I want to start a ski school here and I'll give the local children free lessons, so that we can develop a real skiing community. People will be interested in expanding commercial possibilities, and we'll get enough money to build more adequate tows and lifts. The war won't last forever." Whether or not the council shared his vision made no difference; Pfeifer had seen his future, and he was determined to make it happen.

Benedict, a graduate of the Frank Lloyd Wright School of Architecture, took one look at the rounded hill opposite Aspen Mountain and pictured terraces of homes that would meld into the meadows of sage and scrub oak. The rancher who ran his sheep and cattle along Red Mountain's rim indicated that he might sell his spread when Fritz returned from the war.

Both Benedict and Pfeifer survived the Italian campaign. Benedict telephoned the sheep rancher almost as soon as he stepped off the boat from Italy in 1945. He bought the 600-acre Red Mountain ranch for only twenty dollars an acre and lived at the Hotel Jerome for forty dollars a month, until he could move to Red Mountain. Pfeifer, the victim of a bullet in his lung, convalesced in a Palo Alto hospital, where he poured over mining claims and maps of Aspen Mountain, plotting ways to raise money for his dreamed-of ski runs.

Bil Dunaway, a dynamo from Washington State, celebrated his civilian status by mountain climbing and skiing in and around Chamonix and as-sorted other international ski resorts, and eventually editing *Skiing Magazine* in Denver. In between jobs, he returned to Aspen to ski in a downhill race in 1956, shattered his left leg in the race, and during his recovery decided to buy the *Aspen Times*. He bought it from Vernon Ringle and continues to be its publisher to this day.

Stuart Mace—in charge of the division's dog sled detachment during the war—moved his dogs to Ashcroft in 1948 and became not only a lodge owner and restauranteur, but the unofficial guardian of the upper Castle Creek Valley.

Dick Wright returned to Aspen and became the prototype for the still clas-sic Aspen vocation: contractor in the summer and ski instructor in the winter. He was also president of the Aspen Ski Club.

Johnny Litchfield made an immediate return after the war to Aspen, where he converted Gallagher's Saloon into the famous Red Onion.

Steve Knowlton, a former Olympic skier, made it back to Aspen in 1949, where he and Shady Lane opened the Log Cabin Ski Shop, the forerunner of Aspen Sports. Later Knowlton became the proprietor of the celebrated Golden Horn Restaurant.

Bert Bidwell eventually opened the Mountain Shop, which for a long time remained one of Aspen's premier ski and sport shops. Bob Lewis commenced a distinguished career as a documentary film-maker and environmentalist. Percy Rideout helped found the Aspen Ski School, and Harry Poschman was variously an innkeeper, waiter, potato digger, and wrangler.

The Red Onion and Golden Horn

45

George Tahcowchek, the only Aspen native in the bunch, returned home and eventually worked for the newly formed Aspen Skiing Corporation.

1945: The New Aspen is Born

Throughout the war, Elizabeth Paepcke, like other housewives across the country, lived under the tyranny of rationing. But by the spring of 1945, she had saved enough gasoline coupons for a trip from Chicago to Colorado. After a stop at their ranch near Colorado Springs, she was finally to have an opportunity to show her husband Aspen.

They arrived on Memorial Day. The scenery and the setting were as she remembered — spectacular. But the ambiance lacked the gaiety of her pre-war stay. The only lodging was a somewhat dilapidated Hotel Jerome. The price was right — fifty cents a night — but the food had degenerated to mere refreshments, and the only other restaurant was Gallagher's Saloon. The streets were dusty and deserted. The little Victorian houses were sadly neglected, their gingerbread facades cracked and faded, their owners long since departed. But this was not the Aspen that Walter Paepcke saw.

Paepcke was a man of unusual acumen and vision, as he had proved when he turned his father's modest holdings into the nation's largest packaging company — Container Corporation of America. What he saw was not Aspen's shabby present, but its future potential. Like so many that had come before him, he was captured by Aspen's indefinable magic. To him, its isolation and poverty connoted purity, an environment that could be translated into a serene and exclusive intellectual enclave. As if to prove his instantaneous commitment to this remote Rocky Mountain town, the day after they arrived, he presented his wife with a birthday gift of one of the town's finest Victorian houses. Elizabeth Paepcke, who had not expected this overwhelming reaction to her mountain discovery, was dismayed at the thought of yet another residence to maintain. But Walter's imagination was already in gear, and nothing could stop it now.

In addition to building his corporate empire, Paepcke had long since been involved in the intellectual and cultural life of Chicago. He had received a classical education, first at Chicago's Latin School, and later at Yale. He was deeply influenced by the Greek concept of the complete life: a combination of work, play, and educational leisure. And he and Elizabeth had recently been participants in the Great Books courses, run for captains of industry by Mortimer Adler and University of Chicago Chancellor Robert Hutchins. In the sleepy little hamlet of Aspen, Paepcke saw the ideal setting in which this model of the perfect life might become a reality.

Fortunately for Aspen, the practical side of Paepcke's nature also took hold. In his mind he plotted the improvements that would have to take place before his dream came true. After all, this was a town with no doctor, no laundry, no fire company, bad water, no sewer system, only one hotel, and only one less-than-adequate restaurant. Nothing had been built in Aspen for forty years. But Paepcke had a plan. He met with the townspeople in September 1945 and laid out his "Fourteen Points," through which Aspenites could achieve the good life. The wheels were in motion.

Friedl Pfeifer, discharged from the California hospital where he was recovering from his war wounds, was now in residence in Sun Valley. When he could, he went to Aspen, exploring the claims he had researched on Aspen Mountain and trying to figure out how to get his ski area off the ground. Although Pfeifer tried to get the wealthier citizens of Sun Valley to invest, no one was interested in an unknown mining town in Colorado.

Aspen's first ski school

Paepcke, shuttling back and forth across the country, heard about Pfeifer's schemes. The businessman understood the necessity for an economic base for Aspen and there seemed to be no question that skiing could provide that stability. So he invited Pfeifer to Perry Park, his ranch in Larkspur, to discuss the matter. Pfeifer, whom the Paepckes had never met, arrived at the Larkspur bus station and was duly picked up by one of the ranch hands. Unfortunately, the ranch hand had mistaken Pfeifer for the new stockman. Pfeifer said afterwards that the man kept asking him how he felt about raising turkeys! But the meeting went well. It was clear that while Pfeifer could provide the momentum, Paepcke could provide the money. Although Paepcke himself was not a man of great wealth, he and Elizabeth knew people who were. So, in 1945 the Aspen Skiing Corporation was formed with Pfeifer, the number one shareholder, as the general manager, and George B. Berger, Jr., of Denver as president. Mrs. Paepcke's brother Paul Nitze was the largest investor by far. Other early shareholders were Paepcke, D. R. C. Brown, Jr., William Hodges, Jr., Edgar Hackney of New York, and Robert Collins of Omaha. Actually Nitze, unbeknownst to Paepcke, was a friend of Ryan and Fiske, and had contributed to their earlier schemes for skiers in Aspen.

Aspen's first free shuttle to Lift One

Now Pfeifer could move ahead. All he had to do was figure out who owned what on Aspen Mountain. A total of 863 acres was involved. Eventually, the fledgling corporation obtained leases on 131 acres from the Smuggler-Durant Mine, on 155 acres from the Forest Service, and on the remaining acreage from D. R. C. Brown and Pitkin County.

Meanwhile, in December 1945, true to his word, Pfeifer started his ski school. He was joined by two ex-Dartmouth skiers and 10th Mountain colleagues, Johnny Litchfield and Percy Rideout. Fred Willoughby, recently back from the Army, was elected president of the Ski Club. He and all the rest of the locals and visitors then learned the Arlberg Method that Pfeifer had taught in St. Anton and at Sun Valley.

In between ski lessons, Pfeifer and Willoughby would escort potential investors up Queen's Gulch, past the Midnight Mine, to the Richmond Hill ridge where the Sundeck now stands. Then, with a flourish, they would take off down through Tourtelotte Park, swerving into Roch Run, and finally pouring down almost into the heart of Aspen. That long downhill run, dropping an unprecedented 3,000 vertical feet, was the clincher. Before long, Joseph Hodges, United Air Lines head William Patterson, hotelier Conrad Hilton, and several others joined the Ski Corporation bandwagon.

Starting in the spring of 1946, Pfeifer, the Willoughby brothers, Litchfield, and Rideout began surveying the mountain and developing plans for the lift system and more ski runs. During the summer, the Willoughbys were a hard-working presence, directing the core of paid workers and volunteers. Frank surveyed the lift line, while Fred used a huge bulldozer from the Midnight Mine to clear the old mining roads that zigzagged up the face of the mountain. As a tribute, the switchbacks were dubbed Avenue de Willoughby, and Fred was named the general manager of ski operations for the Skiing Corporation. The first building was the Sundeck restaurant, perched at the crest of Richmond Hill with views in every direction. The lift, built in two sections, went from the top of Aspen Street to the Sundeck. It was finished in December, just in time for the 1946–47 winter season.

Aspen, The Ski Resort

The grand opening of the Aspen ski area was held on January 11, 1947. After a ride up the 15,000-foot chair lift, Colorado Governor Lee Knous gave Elizabeth Robinson, daughter of Aspen's mayor, a starting push-off for the first official run down Aspen Mountain. As a part of the ceremonies, a plaque was presented to the 10th Mountain Division for their "services toward the continuance of mountaineering and skiing." Hundreds of skiers, both visiting and local, tried out the new lifts. It was a long way from the boat tow of the previous winter.

As if to celebrate Aspen's new status, Pfeifer announced that the First Annual Roch Cup Race was to be held in March of that year. As he had hoped, it attracted the nation's top racers and more than enough spectators to fill the 400 beds now available for tourists. Walter Paepcke donated and awarded the silver trophy to combined winner Barney McLean. Competitor Dick Durrance took the occasion to quit his management job at Alta, Utah, and accept the position of Mountain Manager for the Aspen Skiing Corporation. By now, the ranks of the corporation had also been joined by Barney McLean, Bob Perry, and Gordy Wren.

Opening day, 1947

Still, in spite of the progress, in later years Pfeifer was to remember the first few years as something less than glamorous. In actuality, "the longest lift in the world," was actually two lifts. The lower lift went all the way from the bottom to the top of Tourtclotte Park and was built by the same company that built the first lifts at Sun Valley. The upper lift was built out of the timbers from the Park Tunnel mine tram. "We opened up in the middle of December of 1946," said Pfeifer. "At the ski school that first year there were four of us including me; we grossed $3,000. We didn't have any trails except the Roch Run. Spar Gulch was skiable, but barely. And we had no snow and the upper lift was always breaking down."

The beginning of the 1947–48 season saw the arrival of another Aspen legend — the wily and whimsical Swiss skier, Fred Iselin. As co-directors of the ski school, Iselin and Pfeifer combined the best of European and American techniques into something that was eventually called "The Aspen Way." Starting with six instructors, the Aspen Ski School went on to teach thousands of skiers how to realize "the joy of skiing."

Records show that while the Skiing Corporation did make money during those first few years, the profits all went into paying off the capital expenses and improving the mountain. The new shop owners, restauranteurs, and lodge owners had a tough time making ends meet.

The selection of Aspen as the site for the 1950 FIS (Federation Internationale de Ski) World Ski Championships was a turning point. It was the fulfillment of a dream for a small core of Coloradans, who had been quietly lobbying for the event ever since the 1948 Winter Olympics in St. Moritz, Switzerland. And the timing was right: the FIS committee decided that international competitions should be held beyond the confines of Europe. When the officials gave the nod to the United States Ski Association, Pfeifer, Iselin, Durrance, Paepcke, "Ad" Coors, George Berger, and Joseph and William Hodges had already laid the groundwork for choosing Aspen as the Championship site.

When they arrived, teams from all over the world — along with the media, the spectators, and the industry's representatives — were treated to a firsthand experience of Aspen's powdery snow, incredible slopes, and intoxicating atmosphere. By now there was some atmosphere. Litchfield had transformed Gallagher's Saloon into a favorite hangout for visitors and locals alike: the Red Onion. The upper floors of the old Brown and Hoag Building at Cooper and Galena, along with the Paragon Building on Hyman, had been transformed into huge dormitory style lodgings. Steve Knowlton's Golden Horn was open, as was Phil Wright's Country Store. Many of the competitors — such as Andrea Mead, Dave Lawrence, Gale Spence, and Stein Eriksen — came back to Aspen to stay.

At last, Aspen the ski resort was getting the international recognition it deserved. ◗

1950 FIS competitors

The Paepcke Era: 1945–1959

In the years between 1945 and 1950, while Aspen established its reputation as a world-class ski area, Walter Paepcke was earnestly working towards the fulfillment of his personal vision: Aspen as a center of culture. To Paepcke, these two destinies were entirely compatible. Originally Paepcke had a romantic vision of improving the economy through use of native resources: Aspen wood for wood crafts that could be sold; native silver for jewelry; clothes out of wool from Aspen's sheep; and cheese and butter from the cattle.

Walter and Elizabeth Paepcke

But Friedl Pfeifer's enthusiasm for skiing convinced Paepcke and all of Paepcke's moneyed associates that Aspen's greatest resource was snow. So after his role in forming the Aspen Skiing Corporation, Paepcke interested himself primarily in the other company that he had formed at the same time: the Aspen Company.

The Aspen Company

The Aspen Company, which shared many investors with the Aspen Skiing Corporation, was headed by Paepcke, who owned forty-nine percent of the stock. Its purpose was to provide a "community of peace," where Plato's prerequisites for man's complete life could be realized: ". . . where he can earn a living and profit by healthy physical recreation, with facilities at hand for the enjoyment of art, music, and education."

In September 1945 Judge William Shaw helped Paepcke gather together the citizenry in the Pitkin County Courthouse. There, the classic scholar laid out his "fourteen points for the good life." The suggestions were not well received. After all, who was this stranger to be telling Aspen's citizens how to improve their lives and their town? Furthermore, many locals were still hoping for the return of mining. They suspected that Paepcke was a speculator and resented his interference. Nevertheless, there were some who believed that Paepcke's seemingly far-fetched vision might have far-reaching possibilities. The Willoughbys, Laurence Elisha, Mike Magnifico, Tom Sardy, Orest Gerbaz, and the Shaws gave the Chicagoan their support.

One of Paepcke's first steps was to bring Herbert Bayer to Aspen. Bayer, a German architect and graphic designer, had immigrated to the United States just before the war. Already famous as an important interpreter of the Bauhaus movement, Bayer had been retained by Paepcke's Container Corporation in the early forties to produce a number of designs for the company's cutting edge advertisements. Later, Bayer also curated an exhibition of all of the art work produced for the Container Corporation, thus becoming personally acquainted with C.E.O. Walter Paepcke.

Herbert Bayer (r.) with Jose Ortega y Gasset

In early 1946, after Paepcke's fateful discovery of Aspen, Bayer and his wife Joella, who was the daughter of Parisian poet Mina Loy, and their children were living in New York. Bayer had been quite ill, and they were searching for a healthier climate. So Paepcke suggested that Herbert and Joella come visit them in Aspen, giving Bayer a touch of the mountain air that had colored his youth. Sure enough, Bayer felt well enough to go skiing, and he and Joella decided to stay on. To Paepcke, Bayer—the designer, planner, architect, and outdoorsman—was the perfect partner for his transformation of mountain village to cultural retreat. He made Bayer, who continued as a consultant for the Container Corporation, a director of the Aspen Company. While the monetary returns were far less than what he could make as a designer either in Europe or New York, Bayer was intrigued. "I was naïve at the time," said Bayer later, "but naïve ideas are sometimes very powerful." After all, he was being offered a whole town to enhance, restore, and modernize, a task that must have been irresistibly appealing. The Bayers gave in and bought a house from Judge William Shaw, although not at a bargain. Shaw was already a believer, and real estate prices probably took their first jump in fifty years. It was a sign of things to come.

Bayer's first task, with the help of Elizabeth Paepcke and architect Walter Frazier, was to renovate some eighteen houses belonging to the Aspen Company without compromising their Victorian antecedents. Next on the list was the refurbishing of the Hotel Jerome, which the Aspen Company had leased from the Elishas. Bayer brought the plumbing, heating, and electricity up to date, and painted them with a mixture of his own palette and that of the original Victorian decorators. Apparently his taste in colors did not meet with the approval of all the neighbors; one story says that homeowners did not accept Paepcke's offer of free house paint, for fear Bayer would get to pick the colors. Since Bayer's taste did not really run to antiques, his wife Joella furnished the properties with antiques found throughout the valley.

Bayer also supervised the renovation of a number of dormitories for use by prospective skiers, and in his spare time he dashed off designs for the Skiing Corporation's brochures and posters. It was an interesting facet of the career of a man whose paintings would eventually be displayed in museums around the world.

Herbert Bayer and his family put down roots in Aspen. They were full-time residents for many years and summer residents until the late 1970s. As the town grew and various boards and commissions struggled to prevent development from spoiling Aspen's natural assets, Bayer must often have thought back to an Aspen Company meeting in 1946. At that meeting he urged the other directors to buy up what remained of Aspen's core downtown area. By so doing, the Company could influence development around the periphery and could set a particular standard of design from which other developers would take their cue. The purchase would have included all of the land from the Opera House to the foot of the ski slopes. But this bold move was not to be. Walter Paepcke noted, correctly, that the Company did not have that kind of money. It would have cost $150,000.

1949: The Goethe Bicentennial

For all his involvement in Aspen, Paepcke was still the head of a major company in Chicago and still maintained his close ties to that city's intellectual hub, the University of Chicago. In 1948 Paepcke, a trustee of the University, Guiseppe Antonio Borgese, professor emeritus of Italian literature at the University, and Robert M. Hutchins,

The original Music Festival Tent designed by Eero Saarinen

chancellor of the University, conceived a dramatically idealistic plan: to gather together the world's intellectual leaders to celebrate the bicentennial of Goethe's birth. All three men felt that this nineteenth century German poet—who was also a gifted painter, dramatist, critic, and administrator—embodied a faith in man and a spirit of hope that might help to unify both man and world.

The organizing committee decided that, rather than hold the event amidst the hubbub of urban Chicago, they would lure the cognoscenti to Aspen, where there would be fewer distractions. Thus, in addition to the tremendous task of raising money for and organizing the Bicentennial, there was much that needed to be done to ready Aspen for this onslaught. To date, Aspen, while much improved as a tourist town, still had too few guest rooms, no public theatre, and no major auditorium for the orchestral concerts and lectures being planned for the Bicentennial. And from the date of inception, spring 1948, there was less than a year to make ready.

The obvious solution to the problem of a theatre was the renovation of the Wheeler Opera House, which had been gutted by fire in 1912 and was in a still-charred state. Bayer faithfully restored the theatre from early photographs and plans. But an even bolder plan was underfoot for a major auditorium. It was to be a tent, a giant amphitheater under canvas, with sides that would open up to the sun and close down to the rain. The designer was to be the famous architect Eero Saarinen, and the tent would be built on Paepcke's meadowland at the far west end of Aspen's residential district. It would house an orchestra and an audience of up to 2,000 people and cost a princely $55,000.

Through his connections with the musical world, Paepcke engaged the Minneapolis Symphony Orchestra under Dmitri Mitropoulos as the main

54

focus of the Bicentennial Convocation's musical portion. Other performing artists would include Jerome Hine, Dorothy Maynor, Artur Rubenstein, Gregor Piatigorski, Nathan Milstein, Mack Harrell, and Erica Morini. Piatigorski, Milstein, and Rubenstein were not easy to convince; as Jews, they were not certain that they wanted to perform in a festival that celebrated a German. But Walter, as always, was persuasive.

For the intellectual aspects of the Bicentennial, Professor Borgese planned colloquia, panel discussions, and lectures. All of the events would be open to a limited number of ticket holders. The presentations would deal with the significance of Goethe, from the standpoints of his relationship to everything from the natural world to politics. The speakers were among the great minds of the world, ranging from the American playwright Thornton Wilder to the Spanish philosopher and politician José Ortega y Gasset.

But the man who truly drew the attention of the world to Aspen during the summer of 1949 was the legendary humanitarian Albert Schweitzer.

By this date, Schweitzer, a musical and intellectual prodigy in his youth, had already spent thirty-six years ministering to the natives at his jungle hospital in French West Africa at Lambarene. After reading one of his books, Mrs. Paepcke convinced her husband that the reclusive missionary would be the perfect symbol of Goethe's humanitarian spirit. Although Schweitzer seldom traveled, he was lured to the convocation by the offer of $5,000 worth of medicine for his clinic to be donated by Abbott Laboratories. On his one and only trip to the United States, Schweitzer, accompanied by his wife, went first to the University of

Albert Schweitzer in Aspen, 1949

Chicago to speak. Since the correspondence was all from Chicago, he quite naturally assumed that Aspen was quite nearby. Much to his astonishment, he was escorted to a train for a journey of another 1,000 miles. In the early hours of the morning, the Schweitzers were met by Paepcke in Glenwood Springs and escorted to Pioneer Park, the Paepckes' home at the corner of Fourth and Bleeker in Aspen. Breakfast brought further surprises. Appearing as directed at 8 a.m., the bemused guests found not a gracious hostess, but a frantic Elizabeth Paepcke still in her nightgown, struggling to clean up a sudden crisis with the plumbing. Said the good doctor, "Mrs. Schweitzer and I are just in time to witness the second flood."

Mrs. Paepcke recalls some wonderful gatherings at the breakfast table that June, with Dmitri Mitropoulos discussing Bach with Schweitzer, and Thornton Wilder chatting with Dorothy Maynor, her husband (who also stayed with the Paepckes to prevent any possible racial problems at the hotels), and others who dropped by for a cup of coffee.

Pioneer Park

In addition to becoming the Bicentennial Central, Pioneer Park also offered its own valet service. The concert performers, unable to find anyone to press their formal attire, took Mrs. Paepcke at her word when she said she would find someone to take care of the matter. Then she quietly did all the pressing herself. When Arthur Rubenstein gave her twenty-five dollars to pass on to whomever did the work, she simply told him she would see that the money went to the right person.

Guests and speakers unable to stay at the Hotel Jerome were housed in the dormitories and Victorians owned by the Aspen Company, and anyplace else they could find. One speaker slept on a resident's horsehair couch. At first, some of the visitors complained, but they soon discovered that the informal living arrangements promoted a free exchange of ideas. The great and the not-so-great found that chance encounters sometimes sparked more exciting revelations than formal convocations. In the years that followed, these spontaneous discussions became a revered tradition of the Aspen Institute.

Evelyn Ames of Cold Spring Harbor, New York, echoed the sentiments of many of those attending: "At such altitudes, everything was a little sharper, in clearer focus, a little nearer the sky. Here there was no superficially cosmopolitan gathering, no arbitrary elite, but the

Artur Rubenstein rides the chairlift

most surprising, heady brew of Europe and the New World, of Weimar and the corner drugstore, of Goethe and cowboy boots."

Western writer Luke Short (Fred Glidden), already an Aspen resident, said later that when Schweitzer and Thornton Wilder (who also served as Schweitzer's translator) stood together on stage, they "became as one instrument whose only function was to honor a dead German poet."

The entire Goethe Bicentennial cost $250,000. Paepcke had mortgaged his ranch at Larkspur to help pay for it. But by all accounts, the Bicentennial was a great success. And best of all, now the world at large knew Aspen was more than a place for skiing—it was an emerging cultural capital.

Aspen's Cultural Institutions

Following the success of the Goethe Bicentennial, Paepcke immediately set about building on Aspen's new cultural dimension. As a businessman, he was also eager to find ways to use the Aspen Company's accommodations during the eight months outside of the ski season.

Hutchins suggested a kind of university, as did Professor Mortimer Adler. Adler was Hutchins' principal co-worker at the University of Chicago, and together they taught the prestigious two-year Great Books Seminar. Elizabeth and Walter Paepcke had taken the course, as had other future luminaries such as Washington Post publisher Katherine Graham, Illinois senator Charles Percy, and Atlantic Richfield C.E.O. Robert O. Anderson. In response to a query by mail, Ortega y Gasset sent Paepcke a ten-page letter in which he suggested a "High School (Hochschule) of Humanities", in which participants would study current human problems and strive to synthesize the physical and biological sciences with humanities. To do so, they would attend classes, lectures, concerts, and festivals, and would immerse themselves in a "high intellectual and moral milieu."

Already, many of the musicians who played at the Bicentennial had indicated a desire to return to Aspen the following summer, particularly if they could bring their own students with them. They liked the contrast between the solemnity of big city symphonies and the freewheeling ways of Aspen. So Paepcke's Aspen Company purchased the huge lecture tent from the Bicentennial Foundation to use for concerts and agreed to rent the ski dormitories and little Victorians to the visiting musicians and students during the summer.

Next, the Paepckes and Herbert Bayer conceived of a spring conference on design, a place where artists, publishers, architects, engineers, and manufacturers from around the world could come together and discuss the many-faceted world of design. It was organized for the following June.

As for the "Hochschule," no more was done about organizing it until Adler — in the throes of organizing his 54-volume Great Books series — received a phone call from Paepcke in April. Adler joined the Paepckes at the Design Conference to discuss the schedule of lectures to be held that summer, and in so doing, set the pattern for what was soon incorporated as the Aspen Institute for Humanistic Studies. The Institute's first board of directors read like a who's who from six or seven different fields. It included Schweitzer as an honorary director, Ortega y Gasset, Wilder, Hutchins, University of Colorado president Robert Stearns, federal judge and former Colorado governor W. Lee Knous, beer scion Harald Pabst, and several others from industry. John Herron, the son of a respected Aspen mining family, was also asked to join.

Mortimer Adler at an Institute program in the Golden Horn Restaurant

Thus, in the spring of 1950, Walter Paepcke's summer of culture began just weeks after the ski season ended. First on the menu was the June Design Conference. The lecture series and concerts were to follow in July and August, and in fall would be the Photography Conference.

The Design Conference was an immediate success. The visually-oriented participants eagerly accepted the combination of lectures and discussion groups on the relationship of design to contemporary life. Again, the tranquil surroundings seemed to promote the kind of clear thinking that was relevant to urban, as well as rural, settings. And again, attendees and speakers alike found that the casual exchanges amongst each other sometimes produced the most memorable moments. The event's success prompted the 1951 formation of a non-profit corporation called the International Design Conference of Aspen, with its own board of directors and program committee. For the first three years its theme was "Design as a Function of Management." Since 1954 there has been a different theme every year with a distinguished array of speakers participating, including Philip Johnson, Peter Ustinov, Bobby Seale, Betty Friedan, Cornell Capa, Alfred Knopf, S. I. Hayakawa, Josef Albers, Robert Rauschenberg, Gloria Steinem, Ben Shahn, and many more.

The Aspen Music Festival Orchestra performing in the Music Tent

The Music Festival in 1950 featured the Denver Symphony Orchestra and ran for eleven weeks. Soloists included Helen Traubel, Lauritz Melchoir, Mack Harrell, and Vronsky and Babin. And as planned, many of the musicians brought their students with them, filling the ski houses and dormitories with the sounds of strings and brass. The following year, the Festival organized its own orchestra. When it did so, the Festival created a unique opportunity for its young students. In the orchestras, students sat side by side with musicians from the nation's most famous symphony orchestras, allowing them to play with their teachers, as well as under them.

The first official lecture of the Aspen Institute for Humanistic Studies took place in the Wheeler Opera House on July 2, 1950. This lecture and the accompanying seminars were based on Mortimer Adler's Great Books Seminar, as perfected at the University of Chicago. They were stellar events, featuring luminaries such as Reinhold Niebuhr, Karl Menninger, Meredith Wilson, Robert Hutchins, and Clare Booth Luce. But Henry Luce, Jr., the publisher of Time, Inc., pinpointed a fundamental flaw.

After listening to his wife Clare participate in a lecture, he suggested that, instead of just showcasing brilliant lecturers to other members of the intelligentsia, the Institute should focus on businessmen. It was business people who needed the intellectual stimulation if they were to effect change, and they could afford to pay. By mixing with men of letters, theology, government, labor, and science, and by discussing a broad range of fundamental problems, the executives of America's corporations might clarify their own minds to better influence positive change in the world of commerce.

An early Executive Seminar in session

Adler and Paepcke were quick to implement Luce's idea. The first Aspen Executive Seminars were held in 1951 and have continued in essentially the same form to the present day. Thousands of top executives have participated, many calling them a high point in their adult lives.

The year 1950 also brought the first conference for photographers. It was organized, at Paepcke's request, by Ferenc Berko, a native Hungarian photographer who came to the United States just after World War II to teach at the Chicago Institute of Design. With the rebirth of Aspen, he settled in the place as its unofficial photographer in residence. Starting with the Goethe Bicentennial, he created an astonishing chronicle of post-Paepcke Aspen. Although Berko wanted to wait until 1951 in order to plan the Photography Conference properly, Paepcke insisted that it take place in the fall of 1950. The conference was an artistic success, drawing famous photographers such as Eliot Porter, Laura Gilpin, Minor White, Ansel Adams, and Dorothea Lange; but like the Design Conference, it was a financial failure. Paepcke declined to support it for a second year, but it did give rise to Berko's organization of a Screen Classics program for the Institute. Comprising a graphic account of the evolution of film, it is the oldest continuous program of its kind in the United States.

As Paepcke's interests grew—along with the ski trade—it became clear that an airport was needed. So he donated part of his ranchland west of town for an airport, and Commissioner Tom Sardy pushed the project through at the county level. Next, Paepcke had the Institute charter Aspen Airways for daily flights to and from Denver. He also bought back some of the acres near the tent that he had sold to the Aspen Company, and instructed Herbert Bayer to design a building for the new Executive Seminars. It was the true beginning of the Aspen Institute/Aspen Meadows complex, which would take on a distinctive architectural character that became a tribute to the multiple talents of both architects.

Paepcke, although gratified by Aspen's growing popularity, was still a businessman, and he kept an eye on the financial viability of his holdings. In order to capture additional revenue from dining, the Hotel Jerome, leased by Paepcke's Aspen Company, instituted the American Plan. When people demanded the opportunity to eat at Johnny Litchfield's new Red Onion or Steve Knowlton's new Golden Horn restaurants, Paepcke decided to offer a more attractive alternative—the Four Season's Club. Located on Castle Creek at the site of the old Newman mining operation, the Club offered sports as well as food. One of the ponds—filled with ice-cold snowmelt—was optimistically dug out as a swimming pool. There were also tennis courts, grounded with Castle Creek's hard red dirt and surrounded with chicken wire. In the evening, there was dinner and dancing. What there was not was a liquor license. When the city council waffled about granting it to Paepcke, he was outraged and threatened to pull his interests out of Aspen. One disgruntled councilman was heard to say that if that's all it takes to get him out of here, let's do it. But Paepcke's supporters held sway and soon there were drinks at the Four Season's Club too. A short time later, the Jerome Pool was built, and it became Aspen's equivalent to the Algonquin Roundtable. Paepcke even offered visiting luminaries a discount, so that they might act as a draw for the hoi polloi. And it worked. You could spot anyone there: opera singers, Pulitzer prize winners, movie stars, and miners. They might even be drinking together.

Also ensconced in a tiny office at the Hotel Jerome was Robert Craig. Once called one of America's most promising young leaders by *Life Magazine*, Craig arrived in Aspen in 1954 almost broke. On the rebound from a disastrous Himalayan expedition, he bought a little newspaper called the *Aspen Flyer*, which he edited with Peggy Clifford until Paepcke tapped him as the "director" of the Institute. He stayed in that position long enough to see the organization through some dramatic changes and eventually went on to head the Keystone Institute at Keystone, Colorado.

By 1954 Paepcke could look proudly on the success of his three pet projects: the Aspen Institute, the Aspen Summer Music Festival, and the Aspen Music School. The cadre of the seminar leaders were among the most experienced and gifted teachers in the nation. The Festival Orchestra, now composed of instrumentalists who held leading chairs in the best symphony orchestras in the nation, was artistically excellent. And the Music School boasted over 100 summer students. Walter and Elizabeth Paepcke held court at the Hotel Jerome pool, where artists, students, the intelligentsia, and the young ski bums turned-summer-workers mixed freely in a heady cultural atmosphere. The time was ripe for a crisis.

While no one remembers exactly how the dispute started, the leading version states that Paepcke was dissatisfied with the director of the music school and informed him that he would not be engaged for the following summer. The director kept this fact to himself and proceeded to foment an anti-Paepcke movement among the musicians, suggesting that a secession from the Institute was in order. The director hinted that many of the original musicians might be replaced by new people the following summer. When Paepcke learned of the revolution, he was outraged and threatened to withhold use of the tent or Aspen Company housing, should the musicians break with the Institute.

Fortunately, cooler heads prevailed. Cortlandt D. Barnes, Jr., and Nathan Feinsinger, two national patrons of music who maintained second homes in Aspen, negotiated. They proposed a separate organization, in which they and their backers would cover all the operating deficits incurred by the orchestra and the school, if they were still allowed use of the tent and Aspen Company housing. Paepcke accepted the proposal, and the Music Associates of Aspen was formed.

By 1957 Paepcke Auditorium and the Institute's Health Center were completed, and the Meadows complex—including housing, a restaurant, a pool and tennis courts for Institute participants—was under way. Paepcke, still saddened at his loss of the musical portion of his interests, stated that Container Corporation's expansion into the European market mandated that he cut back on his activities in Aspen. He passed the reins to a trustee who had joined the Institute's board in 1953: the brilliant young oilman who would later be president of Atlantic Richfield Oil, Robert O. Anderson.

Three short years later, the man who had used the power of his dreams to build a new Aspen, was dead of cancer at the age of sixty-four. ◆

Aspen Booms Again: 1960–

The changes that Friedl Pfeifer and Walter Paepcke brought to Aspen after the close of World War II created a boom just as revolutionary as the change from Indian hunting ground to mining camp in 1879. The change was slightly more gradual and certainly more long-lived, since Aspen's life as a producing mining camp lasted only fourteen years. But the numbers only told half of the story. After fifty years of having no solid industry to hold the town together, Aspen now had two industries—skiing and culture—that were absolutely blue chip. This fact did not go unnoticed by a number of savvy investors who were determined to get an early piece of the action. By 1960 Aspen itself was a very viable commodity.

Skiing

After the 1950 FIS races there could be no doubt that Aspen was among the premier ski resorts in the world. This was not only due to the terrain, but also to the fine dry powder snow, the brilliant winter sun, and the ambiance of a lovely pastoral town. So, as the Aspen Skiing Corporation continued to improve Aspen Mountain, several individuals quietly concluded that the opportunities were not restricted to one mountain alone.

In 1957 Whipple Van Ness Jones—a Harvard graduate and one-time stockbroker—carved a new ski area out of the Maroon Creek slopes that had once been a favorite ski spot for Aspen's young people in the twenties and

Stein Eriksen's "flip" at Aspen Highlands

thirties. He called the area Aspen Highlands; when it was finished, it had the longest vertical drop of any ski resort in the state. Jones scored another coup when he persuaded the world-famous Norwegian ski champion Stein Eriksen to take over the Aspen Highlands Ski School. Eriksen not only thrilled the crowds with his nordic looks and his daily "flip" off a steep part of the upper slopes, but he also introduced a whole new style of skiing called the "reverse shoulder."

63

A year later Friedl Pfeifer, ever alert to the pulse of the skiing public, saw a perfect chance to develop an area geared towards the beginning and the intermediate skier. After selling his interest in the Ski Corp., he began work on the gentle slopes of Buttermilk Mountain west of town. It was here that the "tiehackers," men who felled the trees to be used as railroad ties and mine props, labored through the hot summers of the 1880s. According to the local legend, by the time their wives trudged up the mountain with their lunches, the milk had inevitably turned into buttermilk; thus the name — Buttermilk Mountain. The first T-bar lift at Buttermilk opened in 1958. In 1963 the area was purchased by the Skiing Corporation and eventually expanded to include Tiehack and Buttermilk West.

Meanwhile, in 1959 D. R. C. Brown, Jr., an Aspen native and son of Aspen pioneer D. R. C. Brown, took the helm of the Skiing Corporation. He proved to be as astute a businessman as his father was. From his offices near the bottom of Little Nell, he ran the Skiing Corporation with one eye on the slopes and the other on the bottom line. Brown was often in the "field," a tall, distinguished figure who once raced in the Roch Cup, seeing for himself how the Ski Corp.'s growing empire was functioning above his father's silent mines.

Snowmass-at-Aspen before development

In the early sixties William and Edwin Janss, brothers from a pioneering land and cattle family in southern California, took a look at the success of the Aspen Skiing Corporation and decided that they would like to develop their own little Colorado ski resort. With their friend and Woody Creek resident Kingsbury Pitcher, they explored most of Colorado. When they finally found what they were looking for, it was the same peak that Pitcher looked at every day from his front yard — Mount Baldy, just eight miles southeast of Aspen, towering over the ranches in Brush Creek.

Professing an interest in cattle ranching, they bought the key ranch at the base of Baldy for $80,000 and quietly acquired the rest of the valley at agricultural prices. In 1964 the Janss Investment Company joined forces with the Aspen Skiing Corporation and began work on Snowmass-at-Aspen. In 1967 the resort opened with five chairlifts, five lodges, two condominiums, and a central Village Mall. Most of it was planned by architect Fritz Benedict, who had developed broad planning expertise and a unique style of contemporary mountain architecture. But by 1968 the Janss' interests had drifted elsewhere, and the resort was sold to American Cement and incorporated as Snowmass American Corporation. In 1977 the Snowmass Land Company bought the company's assets for $7 million. By then Snowmass, still leased from the U.S. Forest Service by the Aspen Skiing Corporation, was the most profitable of the Ski Corp.'s three mountains.

As skiing all over the United States grew in popularity, so did the Aspen Skiing Corporation. In the 1969/70 season it recorded 730,472 skier days on Buttermilk, Snowmass, and Aspen Mountain. By the 1989/90 season that number had expended to 1,121,503. In 1978 the venerable Aspen Skiing Corporation had been sold to Twentieth Century Fox. As one director put it, "It was too good an offer to refuse." By that time, the Corporation owned the ski area at Breckenridge, Fortress Mountain near Banff, Canada, and holdings in Spain. But the sale was the end of an era. Two years later D. R. C. Brown, Jr., retired, leaving others to manage what he had nurtured from a promising natural resource to a vast recreational complex. In 1981 oil mogul Marvin Davis bought Twentieth Century Fox and a few months later sold half of the Skiing Corporation stock to Urban Investment and Development. In 1983 Urban in turn sold to Miller Klutznick Davis and Gray, in which Marvin Davis was a partner, and in 1985 Davis sold the fifty percent he owned as an individual to Bell Mountain Partnership Limited, owned by the Crown family of Chicago.

On December 20, 1986, the Aspen Skiing Corporation opened up the Silver Queen gondola on Aspen Mountain, changing the nature of skiing on a mountain where once mining claims dotted the slopes. Now a skier could reach the top of the mountain in fifteen minutes for his descent on the snowy slopes into Aspen.

Installing the Silver Queen gondola

Through the years, Aspen, Snowmass, Buttermilk, and Aspen Highlands had expanded the skiable acres on their leased land, and all four ski schools had gained reputations as leaders in the field of ski instruction. The inimitable Fred Iselin, who became the head of the Highlands Ski School in 1964, was famous for his free and easy International Method, often comparing his floating style to the flight of a bird. Eriksen, now at Snowmass, continued to promote his "reverse shoulder" method and to demonstrate his gymnastic ability with the famous flip. And at Aspen Mountain, Curt Chase, who was the head of the Aspen Mountain Ski School for over twenty years, made the American Technique one of the foremost skiing methods in the nation. In 1968 teams of ski teachers came to Aspen from all over the world to demonstrate the best and the newest skiing techniques. Then, and in successive Interskis, Aspen's professional teachers scored among the finest in the world.

Subaru Aspen Winternational

Since the 1941 Alpine Championships, when Aspen's sole run could only be reached by a crude boat tow and a long hike uphill, Aspen has been a favorite location for ski races. In 1949 the first Roch Cup was staged, starting a legacy of winners that included Stein Eriksen, Chiharu Igaya, Tom Corcoran, Christian Pravda, Buddy Werner, Billy Kidd, Jimmy Huega, Bobby Cochran, and Peter Luescher. Since 1980 the Roch Cup has been awarded to the winner of America's Downhill, a part of the World Cup series dubbed the Subaru Aspen Winternational.

There were other race series born in Aspen too. NASTAR, the series that allowed amateurs to test their skills running gates, was based in Aspen and operated by former Olympic coach Bob Beattie. Beattie also developed pro skiing through his World Wide Ski Corporation. Aspen's Town Race Series continues to draw an enthusiastic crop of locals who score times that would be impressive for many professionals. Over the holidays, race camps bloom in Aspen. Junior racers continue to be trained through the same ski club that Andre Roch founded in 1937, and through the programs that the Ski Company and the Highlands operate every Saturday for the local children only.

With the opening of Snowmass in the late sixties and the arrival of another persuasive Norwegian named Lars Larson, a second kind of skiing began its resurgence in Aspen — cross-country skiing. Although Aspen's miners would have found it much closer to the sport they knew, Nordic skiing was new to most of modern-day Aspen and America. Spotting a new trend, the developers of Snowmass designed a ski touring center as a part of the resort, and Larson, who had already been converting a few local outdoorsmen, became its enthusiastic director. Purists celebrated the ability to rediscover the quiet of the backwoods in winter, and many non-downhill skiers discovered that cross-country skiing was easy to learn and delightful to practice. It was also less expensive. In 1984 the Aspen/Snowmass Nordic Council was founded to help develop a network of cross-country trails that make up what is now referred to as Aspen's "Fifth Mountain." Over eighty kilometers of trails, maintained by the two towns, now link Aspen to Snowmass. Ashcroft, once the destination of many a miner en route from Leadville on his long "Norwegian snowshoes," is now a privately owned cross-country center with twenty-five kilometers of trails.

In the European tradition, two systems for hut-to-hut skiing were developed in the Aspen area for the more adventurous winter travelers. The Braun Hut System, named after mountaineer Fred A. Braun who founded Aspen's mountain rescue team, started with the Tagert Hut in the 1950s, and now offers six huts for backcountry skiing between Aspen and Crested Butte. The 10th Mountain Trail Association was created in 1980 by Aspen architect Fritz Benedict, planner Elizabeth Holekamp Boyles, and a group of volunteers, and was named after Benedict's old division. This backcountry system run by 10th Mountain is located in the mountains between Aspen, Vail, and Leadville, and consists of over 300 miles of trails that connect about twenty huts, lodges, and inns.

The Cultural Legacy

Ever since Mrs. Gillespie's cultural evenings in Aspen's largest tent in 1880, Aspen has been receptive to the more civilized aspects of life. Throughout its days as a booming mining city, and even into the quiet years, Aspen's citizens tenaciously continued to attend concerts, lectures, and theatrical productions whenever they were offered.

Walter Paepcke's vision brought a new level of intellectual and cultural pursuits to Aspen in the summer. And with them came new audiences. Those giving the lectures and the concerts brought their families and invited their friends. Others came especially for the concerts or the lectures or the Design Conference, and returned for no excuse at all, enchanted with the clean-smelling mountain air, the incredible scenery, the Victorian gingerbread, the mellowed brick buildings, and the amazing mix of people.

Among the first well-known artists to establish a presence in Aspen were Mr. and Mrs. Richard Dyer-Bennett. Dyer-Bennett was nationally established as a folk singer and recording artist when he and his wife first visited Aspen in the forties. In 1949, just before the Goethe Bicentennial, at Paepcke's suggestion, they moved their School of Minstrelsy and Dance to Aspen and began holding classes in Fritz Benedict's ranch barn on Red Mountain. A variety of individual craftspeople and other artists soon settled in Aspen, eager to experience the creative atmosphere and to sell their wares to the affluent tourists. Galleries sprang up, along with a sprinkling of shops that offered the beautiful and the unusual made by local and distant craftspeople.

In the sixties, "art" came to Aspen in a big way. To complement the burgeoning number of art galleries, the Institute's new president Alvin Eurich established a significant art program. An exhibition of painting by Willem de Kooning was mounted in 1965, and soon after, John Powers, who was an Institute board member and former president of Prentice Hall Publishing, put together an important exhibit of early Pop Art. In 1967 Powers and fellow art collectors Armand Bartos and Larry Aldridge organized the Aspen Center for Contemporary Art (ACCA). Until 1970, under the ACCA's aegis, the nation's most exciting contemporary artists spent a few summer months in the ramshackle studios on the upper floor of the old Brand Building, then owned by R. O. Anderson. They included Robert Indiana, Les Levine, Alan D'Arcangelo, Robert Morris, Claus Oldenburg, DeWain Valentine, James Rosenquist, Robert Rauschenberg, and Roy Liechtenstein. Oldenburg, gazing at the towering mountains from the balcony of an art gallery, was heard to say mournfully that nature made him nervous. Levine managed to get himself hauled into the police station when the anti-hippie police force was taking shaggy-looking people in for "loitering." The artists were a revelation to Aspen, and they added another piquant facet to the town's already eclectic population.

The demise of the Aspen Center for Contemporary Art, primarily because of the lack of studio space, did not bring the movement to an end. Many artists continued to live and work in Aspen.

Anderson Ranch was one of the seven working ranches located in the Brush Creek Valley before the Janss brothers bought the property. In 1966, as they planned their new Snowmass Resort, they asked ceramicist Paul Soldner, a nationally known Aspen artist, to choose one of the ranch sites for a community arts center. Soldner chose Anderson Ranch, not only for its mellow log barns and farmhouse, but also for its spectacular view. By 1968 it had been renovated for use as an arts center by Colorado Mountain College. In 1973 the resort's owners, the Snowmass American Corporation, turned operation of the property over to a board of community leaders. The group incorporated as the Snowmass Arts Foundation. Its mission was to develop a nationally prominent summer arts school. Soon after, the foundation officially became the Anderson Ranch Arts Foundation and School. Now, the buildings that once housed hay and sheep, host resident artists and students from all over the country. The Ranch offers up to eighty summer workshops, including photography, ceramics, furni-

Paul Soldner

ture making, print making, sculpture and painting, and interdisciplinary studies. In recent summers, nearly a thousand students have participated in workshops. Artists-in-residence work on their own projects through the winter months, and in the summer help to teach classes.

By 1979 there were many Aspenites who felt that the city's broad interest in the arts merited a permanent art museum. Through the cooperative efforts of the city, the county, and the citizenry, the old Holy Cross Electric Building at the foot of Mill Street was transformed into the Aspen Center for the Visual Arts. The Center was conceived as a vehicle for changing exhibitions rather than a permanent collection, and it opened in June 1979 with a show of works by Willem De Kooning, Andy Warhol, and Robert Rauschenberg. Since that time, the museum—it is now the Aspen Art

Museum—has brought a wide variety of art to Aspen, from the traditional to the controversial. Its spacious riverside grounds feature annual exhibitions of site-specific outdoor sculpture and several permanent sculptures.

Dance became another important aspect of Aspen's cultural offerings in 1969. Encouraged

Students at the Aspen Center for Visual Arts

by the burgeoning artistic community in Aspen, and looking for new audiences, William F. Christensen of Salt Lake City's Ballet West tried a bold experiment—he brought his company to Aspen for the summer. Although the elementary school gymnasium was as close as Aspen could get to a stage and an auditorium, Ballet West was an instant success. The company's mix of classical ballet with just a touch of the modern was perfect for those who had left ballet performances behind in big cities, and for those who had never before seen a ballet performance. In spite of music on tape and improvised sets, the town was hooked. The dancers, with their distinctive walks and inevitable dance bags, became another part of the Aspen scene. Locals loved it when the dancers unwound after performances at the downtown discotheques. Dance had come to Aspen for good.

As the audiences became more sophisticated, so did the productions. In 1981 the board of Ballet West in Aspen decided to expand the program into a festival that would include other companies, and the name was changed to the Ballet Aspen Festival. Today the organization is called DanceAspen and brings a wide variety of companies to Aspen for summer performances, for intensive summer workshops for ballet students, and for a variety of educational activities. Several other dance companies, some made up of local performers, offer programs throughout the year.

Theater has always been an Aspen tradition. Since the Corkhill Opera House opened in 1881, a scant two years after the first tent went up in Aspen, the town has been a regular stop for a variety of touring companies. With much fanfare, the Wheeler Opera House opened in 1889 to a steady bill of dance, opera, chamber music, theater, vaudeville, and minstrel shows. After the Wheeler was gutted by fire in 1912, what dramatic productions there were took place in makeshift theaters. The interior of the Wheeler was completely renovated under Herbert Bayer's direction in the late forties. Bayer unearthed the original drawings for the building and followed them as closely as possible. The exterior was restored in 1974, and ten years later the city purchased the Wheeler, and bonds were passed to finance a complete renovation.

Today the stage again hosts a wide variety of productions, including one or more musicals produced by the Aspen Community Theatre with local talent. In the theater tent in the Art Park at the bottom of Mill Street, the Aspen Theatre Company presents several plays every summer featuring actors and actresses from Aspen. The Snowmass/Aspen Repertory Theatre brings professional thespians to Snowmass every summer to star in several plays presented in repertory style.

The Aspen Music Festival was an unqualified success from the very beginning and continued to be so. There are now four primary orchestras that perform throughout the summer, as well as scores of master classes, chamber concerts, and student concerts. Eero Saarinen's orange and white tent was replaced in 1964 with a tent designed by Herbert Bayer. In recent summers, more than 100,000 people annually have attended concerts at the tent and at the Wheeler Opera House.

In 1964 Robert O. Anderson, who had come into possession of the lovely old Four Seasons Club on Castle Creek, gave the property to the Music Associates as a campus for the Music School. Presently, the school hosts over 900 students each summer from every part of the world and prides itself on support

The Aspen Wind Ensemble in Paepcke Park

for new music in its concert programing. In addition to instrumental, composition, conducting, and vocal studies, the school offers a Choral Institute, a Center for Advanced Quartet Studies, the Edgar Stanton Audio Recording Institute, the Opera Workshop, the Center for Compositional Studies, and a thriving Conference on Contemporary Music.

The Aspen Institute for Humanistic Studies, in the meantime, underwent a number of changes after the Paepcke era. Robert O. Anderson, after he took over from Paepcke in 1957, make it clear that the Institute would no longer attempt to be a civic focal center for the town of Aspen. He was already busy moving the Institute into the international sector, while striving to establish new and meaningful programs at home.

The Aspen Institute for Humanistic Studies

By 1963 the Institute's Meadows complex was complete. It included with Paepcke Auditorium, the distinctive octagonal Seminar Building, the Health Center, the Aspen Meadows Restaurant and Lodge complex, the pool (which later was covered with a geodesic dome designed by Buckminster Fuller), and the tennis courts. The entire complex was meant to enhance the Institute's basic concept — to provide the opportunity for reflective thought in an aesthetic environment that attended to both intellectual and physical needs. After the trials and errors of the first year, the Institute's method remained constant: to gather thoughtful men and women around a table to converse with one another, to explore the great literature of the world, and to translate ideas into acts suitable to the challenges of our age.

While this intellectual portion was an immediate success, the physical side took a little longer. The lovely Health Center — reputed to have the best staff in the nation — was often completely empty. The executives of the fifties and early sixties did not believe in the value of exercise. However, once use of the facility became a part of the tuition fees, the program caught on, and participants found that classes served to break down barriers and create more casual exchanges. Director Tage Pedersen, formerly the head of all of the YMCAs in Denmark, worked out a program of exercise that avoided monotony and included lots of laughter. Many executives later attested that the Health Center provided the high points of the Institute experience.

Gradually, the Institute expanded the scope of its interests to such an extent that the name was changed from the Aspen Institute for Humanistic Studies to the broader, Aspen Institute. It now sponsors programs in two major groups: seminars and policy. The seminar programs include the Executive Seminars, Justice and Society Seminars, Communications and Society Seminars, and the Corporation in Contemporary Society Seminars. The policy programs focus on major emerging challenges to national and international leadership. They have include programs on Asia, Indochina, Hispanic-Americans and the business community, policy issues in energy and resources, and rural economic policies.

In the late seventies, the Aspen Institute made another major change — headquarters for the organization were moved to New York. The move allowed president Joseph Slater and his staff closer contact with the leaders of industry and commerce, which was advantageous for both the recruitment of participants and for fundraising. In 1980 headquarters moved again; this time it was to the Wye Plantation on the eastern shore of Maryland. Donated by Arthur Houghton, Wye was close to Washington, D.C., and provided a huge estate that could be used year-round for seminars. Soon after, permanent facilities were also established in Berlin and Rome, and an Institute presence was established in Sweden, France, Italy, Great Britain, and Japan.

Aspen continues to be the site of summer seminars and of special events, such as the Institute's fortieth anniversary, at which United States President George Bush and British Prime Minister Margaret Thatcher were given the Institute's Distinguished Statesman Award, given only twice before in the Institute's forty-year history.

The Aspen Center for Physics was spawned by the Institute in the early sixties. In 1961, two physicists approached Institute director Robert Craig with an intriguing idea. The scientists, George Stranahan of Carnegie Institute of Technology and Michael Cohen of the University of Pennsylvania, proposed a unique sort of research center where theoretical physicists might gather in the summer. It would be an unstructured environment, free of distractions, where a physicist might work unfettered by the normal responsibilities of classrooms and corporations. Up to this point, the eleven-year-old Aspen Institute had concentrated primarily on bringing together scholars and business people to study the Great Books. But since its original mission called for synthesizing the sciences with the humanities, Craig received the suggestion with enthusiasm and brought the concept to the Chairman of the Board Robert O. Anderson.

Anderson immediately formed a committee of eminent physicists to discuss the prospect, and the group moved with remarkable speed. Working with the basic concept proposed by Stranahan and Cohen, the committee agreed that the Aspen Institute would supply housing for the participants, while they in turn would depend on summer salaries from their own institutions or fellowships for their upkeep. Anderson made several acres of the Aspen Institute's campus available and commissioned Bauhaus architect Herbert Bayer to design and oversee construction of a physics building. By summer of 1962 the building, funded by the Needmor Foundation, was complete. In 1968 the Physics Division became an independent non-profit corporation called the Aspen Center for Physics. Today—structured much as Stranahan and Cohen envisioned it, and funded by many laboratories, corporations, and foundations—the Center has a world-wide reputation as a unique environment for the pursuit of basic scientific knowledge. Participants are free to work at their own speeds in their own ways, allowing collaborations to occur spontaneously, often across lines of specialization.

During its fifteen-week summer session, the Aspen Center for Physics now hosts a total of 400 physicists (no more than eighty at one time) from about 100 institutions. Three intensive winter conferences are held at the Center, and programs on subjects of special concern to the scientific community are held before and after the summer session. Several Nobel Laureates have done work at the Center, including Richard Feynman, Philip Anderson, James Cronin, Murray Gell-Mann, Leon Lederman, and Hans Bethe, who gave part of his prize money to the Center. The Physics Center Lecture Series has become a summer tradition, elucidating the phenomena of the physical world for the non-scientific public. ◗

Mathematical Foundations Rock
Aspen Center for Physics

Growth and Politics

The growth that took place in Aspen in the forty years between 1960 and the end of the century was nothing short of phenomenal. The population of the city itself increased more than 500%, going from 1,101 in 1960 to 6,222 in 1998. The population of Pitkin County, an oddly shaped territory that encompasses 960 square miles and the townships of Basalt and Redstone, went from 2,381 in 1960 to 14,118 in 1998, a testament to the inexorable spread of humanity beyond the western edges of the city and into the rural communities of Basalt and Carbondale. As one weary community activist put it, "A valley less loved would have been ruined."

To some, it was as though the town's whole ethos had changed. Long-time Aspen watcher Peggy Clifford wrote that in 1953 Aspen had "no paved streets, stoplights, central heating, best sellers, supermarkets, traffic jams, air pollution, crime or juvenile delinquency. But it had two bookstores and Aspen shops sold Venetian glass, Irish sweaters, Pucci dress, Gucci leathers and Andy Warhol drawings long before they became status symbols." [1] But by the end of the century, some thought that the desire for civilization had passed into full-blown commercialization. Roomy, contemporary chain stores—glossy and clean—had replaced many of the funky, independent shops and the backwoods were filled not only by hikers, but by hikers with cell phones.

In the forties and fifties, said Clifford in her book, *Aspen: Dreams and Dilemmas*, "...no one thought much about growth and progress in Aspen. Success, to Aspenites, was qualitative, not quantitative. The natives, who had stayed in Aspen through the lean years, simply liked living there. It was beautiful, it was serene, and it was their home. The people who moved there after the war came for a variety of reasons, but none of them had to do with success. Indeed, many of the new citizens had deliberately turned their backs on lucrative futures in big cities. They were mavericks who had concluded at some point that they were not interested in the things

Locals on Mill Street, early sixties

most Americans were interested in: comfort, convenience, affluence, big cars, bigger houses. If they had been interested in those things, they certainly would not have come to Aspen where the predominant life style was living gracefully on a shoestring." [2]

Until 1955 and 1956 respectively, Aspen and Pitkin County had no zoning laws. Passing them at all was a struggle. Many of the natives, sensing only the possibilities of growth, failed to see the value of more rules and regulations. A few free thinkers, displeased with the portion of the code that permitted billboards along the scenic Highway 82 to Aspen, appointed themselves as aesthetic vigilantes and simply cut them down under the cover of darkness.

For those who travel Aspen's byways today, it is hard to imagine that for years Aspen's residents and visitors trod the streets through a miasma of dust in the summer, mud in the spring, and slush in the winter. Although Main Street—as a part of a state highway—was paved in 1954, it was not until 1967 that Aspen's downtown and then its residential streets were paved, mostly at a cost to homeowners rather than to the city. The road over Independence Pass, the fastest way to Leadville and points east, had sustained heavy travel consistently since the first prospectors found their way over its heights in 1879. However, until the early 1970s, it also remained unpaved. Nevertheless, even with their boots in the dust, the veterans of the "Quiet Years" were ready to move on, even if on dirt roads.

The year 1960 seemed to be the real start of Aspen's second boom. One reason was the sudden spurt in the popularity of skiing. What had been essentially an elitist sport, suddenly became the newest rage for the newly affluent middle class. People took to the slopes in unprecedented numbers. In only one year, from 1959 to 1960, the number of out-of-state skiers who visited Colorado doubled from 75,000 to 140,000.

The celebration of Winterskol in Aspen

A second reason was simple—Aspen had become chic. Visiting Aspen became a prestigious experience. Aspen resident Fred Glidden (renowned as the western writer Luke Short) said the inhabitants were right out of Fitzgerald, golden people whose appetites were as extraordinary as their charms. Later, writer Peggy Clifford explained further: "Aspen's dazzling setting, its freewheeling style, its originality, its clever mix of art and sport made it singularly desirable. Because it was out of step, it was in vogue. . . America was full of rebels now, but Aspen's rebels were . . . nice. They were healthy. They enjoyed sports and art and had no interest at all in rousing the rabble. But as affluent America adopted Aspen, Aspen debated the merits of affluence." [3]

In no way were the zoning regulations of 1955 adequate for the building that began in 1960, although consultant Trafton Bean had succeeded in mandating the deep setbacks that avoided strip development along Highway 82. Out-of-town developers were among the first to take advantage of Aspen's new cachet. Many locals followed suit. Before the city fathers knew it, scores of condominiums—the strange, new phenomena—were blossoming everywhere. Large new buildings began to take over neighborhoods. Employees who had lived above shops found themselves homeless in the wake of one more condominium. Sensing the wave of the future, the Chamber of Commerce opened a full-time office with a reservation service, commissioned a national advertising campaign, and discussed hiring an agency to solicit conferences for the town.

In 1962, for the first time, a newcomer took over city hall. Up to that time town officials had been considered functionaries and public servants, not politicians and power brokers. After all, for many years Mayor Wagner had been famous chiefly for keeping the water ditches free of debris. Now, Harald "Shorty" Pabst—scion of the beer family, an Institute trustee, and an Aspen Skiing Corporation director—began to pave the way for a glossier, more luxurious Aspen. In 1965 Dr. Robert "Bugsy" Barnard, Shorty's chief opponent on the city council, wrested power from Pabst. Pabst retaliated by starting the *Aspen Illustrated News*, a venue in which he could have his own editorial voice.

Harald "Shorty" Pabst

In 1966 an Aspen Area Master Plan was adopted in an effort to guide the region's growth pattern. By now the town had doubled in size since 1960 and the county had tripled. But it was hoped that the Master Plan and newly establishing planning and zoning boards would guide Aspen safely

"Hippies" arrive in Aspen

between runaway growth and reasonable prosperity. Understandably, there was some disagreement about what reasonable growth and reasonable prosperity was. It became more and more difficult to tell the good guys from the bad guys. What did not change was Aspen's reputation as an "anything goes" sort of place. Word of Aspen's beauty and freedom reached a whole generation of what the media dubbed "hippies," and in the summer of 1967 they arrived in Aspen in droves. Alarmed by the increasing quantities of shabby young people wandering around downtown Aspen, sometimes "spare changing" the more prosperous citizens, some of the local businessmen went to the city council to ask for a crackdown. The result—fully endorsed by the mayor, the city council, the police, and the sheriff—was the resurrection of an old vagrancy ordinance that prohibited "blocking the sidewalk." Policemen started rounding up longhairs with daisies behind their ears and bringing them to court. The city magistrate, a conservative Swiss restaurateur, gave one youth ninety days in jail and a $300 fine for sitting on the sidewalk.

In typical Aspen style, another group of outraged citizens, as liberal as the judge and his cohorts were conservative, reorganized Aspen's chapter of the American Civil Liberties Union to protest the treatment of the hippies. *Times* editor Bil Dunaway sided with the Civil Liberties Union, and *Illustrated* editor Shorty Pabst sided with the businessmen. Joe Edwards, a young lawyer from Texas, filed suit against the City of Aspen in the Federal Court in Denver. The federal judge issued a strong warning to the city to improve the situation, or else: The magistrate was fired, and a year later the hippie movement quietly disappeared. With the hippies went Pabst and Barnard's imperial style of city management.

In 1969 Eve Homeyer, a local business owner, defeated Joe Edwards by a six-vote margin in the race for mayor. Although Edwards alarmed some of the citizenry with his no-growth politics, he represented the beginning of a slow but powerful movement. The following November, in a rebellious action typical of Aspen's contrary and sometimes cranky liberals, "outlaw" journalist Hunter Thompson ran for sheriff in a widely publicized cam-

paign. He lost the race to the incum-
bent—a lanky, taciturn cowboy—but
the passion and anger exhibited by his
supporters was a sign of the division
between those who wanted Aspen to
remain as it had been, innocent and un-
spoiled, and those who wanted to share
its glory with an ever-growing population of newcomers.

The 1970s ushered in a period of development in which the focus of attention was centered on planning for the
Aspen of the future. In 1970 ground
was broken for the Aspen Airport
Business Center (AABC), located several miles east of Aspen along Highway 82. The brainchild of entrepreneur
John McBride, the office park was a

More living units for Aspen

radical idea at the time, and was approved only after months of wrangling
with the county planning and zoning commission. The chief stumbling
block was a plan for a large Safeway store at the Business Center. Twenty
years later downtown merchants, besieged with complaints about parking
problems and traffic, might have welcomed the idea, but at the time they
worried that it would take business away from the core area. Approval for
the Business Center came only after McBride gave up the supermarket.
The AABC quickly became a Mecca for small non-retail oriented businesses that could not afford the ever-escalating commercial rents in downtown Aspen. Today it houses 130 businesses and 120 condominium units
in the office park. At the turn of the century an additional 60 houses, 12
townhomes, and the Aspen area branch of Colorado Mountain College
were also added.

The new mayor Eve Homeyer ran a tight ship, but Aspen was still Aspen.
City council meetings were never long except when the subject was dogs
or the Olympics. On the first subject, the council finally laid down the law
to pet owners who wanted a policy of *laissez faire* for their dogs too, and
ruled that packs of wild dogs could not roam the city unleashed. On the
second issue, to the horror of the rest of the ski world, Aspen voted against
allowing Winter Olympic events to be held on Aspen Mountain in 1972,
insisting that the town's infrastructure could not sustain Olympic-size
crowds. In fact, complained some of the old-timers, the usual crowd of
"liberals" were just showing off their ability to turn down what every other
ski resort was dying for.

During Eve Homeyer's four-year tenure as mayor, she and her city council—which ran the gamut from very liberal to very conservative—managed to rack up a considerable number of accomplishments which set the stage for the next several decades. The first full-time city planner was hired and a total of 230 acres was bought with city funds to be used for parks. The open space issue came to a head soon after the North of Nell building at the base of the ski hill on Durant was completed. Although it is now dwarfed by the huge St. Regis Hotel, at the time its height and mass radicalized the town. When it was discovered that land in the dead center of town, across from Wagner Park, was also slated for a giant condominium project, in less than 10 days the indomitable Mayor Homeyer collected private philanthropic pledges for more than $100,000 towards purchase of the property that was to become the Rubey Park downtown bus station. Total purchase price of the property was $300,000. Today, that prime downtown property would be worth millions.

Next, following the vote to become a Home Rule city, the council passed the sixth penny sales tax for open space which permitted them to buy the golf course land for $2 million and thirty acres of land near the water plant. The council also put a down payment on the Rio Grande property between the Hotel Jerome and the Roaring Fork River. A seventh penny tax provided for transportation, the forerunner to what would eventually become the Roaring Fork Transit Authority (RFTA). The city also established a series of six view planes that could not be compromised by new building projects, thus limiting height, if not mass.

In 1972 Edwards and another young attorney, Dwight Shellman, were elected county commissioners. They joined Commissioner J. Sterling Baxter, a local physician who had ruled the county with Tom Sardy and Clyde Vagneur. Sardy, the local undertaker and co-owner with Walter Paepcke of the Aspen Lumber and Supply, had decided to retire after almost two decades in office. Vagneur, a down-home conservative, was from a family that had pioneered ranching in the valley. Now, with a majority of votes, Edwards and Shellman were determined to have their way with the county, with or without the help of Dr. Baxter.

Shellman, Baxter, and Edwards

In 1973 bartender-cum-ski area consultant Stacy Standley succeeded Homeyer as mayor. He was of one mind with Edwards and Shellman. Their objective was simple—to enact legislation that would control growth, and for the short term to "control" meant to "limit." And "limit" they did. Together, they influenced a host of actions that forced builders of anything from a single-family dwelling to a multi-use development to comply with an increasingly complex set of zoning regulations. Battle lines were drawn. It was Business versus Beauty, Idealists versus Greedheads, and Obstructionists versus Common Sense. Name calling was rampant. You were either for growth or against it. But the new order was in office and they didn't hesitate to use their power for what they believed to be the public good—controlling growth and doing it in a hurry. All building permits were held in abeyance pending a tightening of city zoning regulations.

Hyman Street just before work on the mall begins

In an effort to solve the traffic problem and to preserve some of the atmosphere in downtown Aspen, a plan for a mall was passed. Purchase of the Rio Grande property was completed. And the Commissioners rezoned the entire county; now instead of a quarter-acre per house, in some cases land was zoned for thirty acres per house. The proposed two-block mall was a radical concept designed to return the downtown streets to walkers. It was several years in the planning stages—subject, as usual, to outraged naysayers. But once it finally opened in 1976, it gave Aspen's historic downtown a whole new dimension. No one could say it was a restoration of things past, but visitors and residents alike clearly enjoyed the return to the camaraderie of strolling or people-watching in the park-like environment. By the end of the century, retail space in the mall was at a premium and all notions of "too far to park your car" were dismissed as non-problematic.

Plans were also made for an extensive trail system (masterminded by Fritz Benedict and his architectural firm), for the creation of more parks, and for expanded green space around the town's periphery. A new hospital and a new airport were planned. There had always been a hospital in Aspen; the first was built with miner's contributions in 1891. In 1958 the old Citizen's Hospital was torn down and a new one was built in its place at the base of Red Mountain. Now, in 1977, a hospital district and a bond issue produced a sophisticated forty-nine-bed facility on Castle Creek, appropriate to the growing demands of a more sophisticated population.

In spite of dire predictions from the commercial community, business boomed. In fact, downzoning served to make property in Aspen even more attractive, and far more expensive. To the dismay of those who wanted to "save" Aspen, "selling" Aspen became more and more desirable. After saving the land so that ranchers could live in peace, many ranchers chose to sell their land so they could live in luxury.

Even a disastrous no-snow year in 1976 could not stem the tide. Clean, beautiful, eccentric, and pleasure-loving Aspen was where the elite wanted to be. In 1977 a new City/County Growth Management Plan was implemented, limiting growth to 3.4 percent annually. Although growth was slowed, a unexpected side effect of the policies of Aspen's no-growth legislators began to make itself felt and the pain was to last into the new millennium. As building slowed, prices rose. As prices rose, the old "buyers" were forced out, making way for new "buyers" for whom there was "no price resistance." Housing, in particular, became an ever-escalating problem. As building stopped, rents of existing spaces rose. And no matter how shabby, they were snapped up by wealthy newcomers who could afford to pay whatever landlords asked. By 1978, with nowhere to live, the snowbirds, Aspen's traditional worker base, flew elsewhere leaving the resort dangerously short of workers. In desperation, the city and the county began to consider inducements towards the building of low-cost housing. By 1979 the cost of living in Aspen was higher than any other city in the continental United States. And for the first time in the hundred years since B. Clarke Wheeler laid out the town's configuration just slightly off of magnetic north, downtown reached beyond its unofficial Main Street border clear down to the Roaring Fork River. ❧

Aspen Enters a New Century

By the early 1980s, it was undeniably clear that the Aspen "boom" was not a fluke. Short of putting a gate across Highway 82 that said "No More New Residents Permitted" (and the idea was discussed with some seriousness) there was no way to stop the flow. The immediate attraction was evident: an incredibly beautiful valley in the heart of some of the earth's finest ski country. But newcomers were drawn for far more complicated reasons. Urbanites and suburbanites all over the county were evincing a longing for "community," for the sense of belonging that a small town might deliver. Aspen was a small town with big city sensibility. The grocery clerks knew you. You could call the city manager directly and get him to fill the pothole on your street. Your kids were safe walking home from the bus stop. And you could be "someone" who got written up in the newspaper, even if it was just as a volunteer on a fund-raising committee. On the other hand, there was no small town insularity—none of the provincial prejudices common to those who had never gone beyond their own backyards. Aspenites were educated and traveled. The guy pumping gas could have his Ph.D. Your "hippie neighbor" was the heir to Alcoa Aluminum. There was gossip, but it wasn't "small town gossip" about who the kindergarten teacher was dating. It was more like who was sailing his Hobee Cat across the Pacific during the off-season.

Specific reasons for migrating to the Roaring Fork Valley were specific to your life circumstance. For young, middle-class families Aspen and the valley provided a beautiful environment, a healthy life style, good schools, the opportunity to get involved in your community in a meaningful way, and innumerable things to do besides watch TV and visit the mall. For the very rich there was a semblance of community, there was every luxury money could buy—from 5-star restaurants to a branch of Cartiers, there were endless opportunities for recreation, and finally, there were plenty of other "very rich" against whom you could compete with impunity. For the famous there were all of the advan-

The Little Nell Hotel experience

The annual "uphill" race on Aspen Mt.

tages accorded to the rich, plus undeniable cache, a greater chance of being able to walk the streets like a normal person (a real Aspenite would *never* stoop to asking for an autograph), and, of course, the chance to hang out with *other* famous people and with the very rich people, whom the famous also needed and liked. And finally, sportsmen and sportswomen found a heaven of non-team action sports from fly-fishing to 100-mile megamarathons to skate boarding *down* Independence Pass to *uphill* skiing. This was *serious* sports country where many men and women lived only to exercise.

In short, people were going to keep on coming. Meanwhile, in spite of the 1977 Growth Management Plan and the far more comprehensive Community Plan of the nineties, there was not then, and probably would never be, consensus around the issue of growth. The pro-growth factions would always want to exploit the population boom to varying degrees and the preservationists would always want to preserve everything that brought them to Aspen in the first place. Furthermore, once an individual had a foothold in the valley, he or she often demonstrated a definite tendency towards BANANA, a local irony that went well beyond its original status as a joke: *"Build Absolutely Nothing Anywhere Near Anybody."* The attitudes between the "I've got mine, now the heck with the rest of you," and the "I'm going to get mine no matter what the cost to the rest of you" often seemed to put lawmakers and appointed boards in an impossible position.

Luxury Living for the Few

If they could not stop growth, most residents of Pitkin County agreed that they at least wanted to "control" growth. The 1977 City/County Growth Management Plan was only the beginning. By the 1980s the zoning commission members had become serious players in deciding Aspen's future. Pitkin County became nationally renown for the difficulty of getting pro-

84

jects passed, and even single-home owners took to hiring former planning department staffers as consultants in getting a new addition through the notorious "P & Z." "It didn't stop the developments," said one former city council member, " but it did prevent more egregious mistakes like the huge, ugly condominium blocks that went up in the seventies, and it forced builders to set aside space for employees at a price that employees could afford." Although nothing short of Historic Designation could prevent "tear-downs," (homes that were purchased for the value of the lot, and then completely demolished to make way for a new structure), to some degree the P& Z could and did control the size and design of homes, forcing them to fit into the surrounding neighborhood.

Bulldozing a Victorian

Some new structures were merely luxurious single-family homes that were inserted, without much comment, into the old neighborhoods that had once sported chickens and milk cows in the back yards. Others, in the "pocket palace" development on the once rural Ute Avenue, were chiefly remarkable for immense square footage on tiny lots. The day of hiding your wealth is over, declared the real estate community.

Other projects, while outwardly built to serve the needs of well-heeled tourists, were clearly a tremendous asset to the entire community. In 1981, after years of financial struggle, Jerome B. Wheeler's original Hotel Jerome got a new owner with deeper pockets and underwent a comprehensive face-lift. By 1988 the grand old lady of Aspen re-emerged as one of Aspen's most luxurious lodging places with a new wing, a new pool, a new patio, a new ballroom, and a new look of classic Victorian elegance.

Reopening of the Hotel Jerome; John Denver, Elizabeth Paepcke, Hildur Anderson, Andy Mill, Bill Stirling

The Skiing Company's luxury hotel at the base of Little Nell was much disputed as too much, too big, but once it was completed most Aspenites seemed to take pride in having a really first-class new hotel, and were often seen having tea on the terrace or drinks in the bar. With its prime location and spacious plaza, it quickly became an integral part of downtown. In 1999, a statue honoring the 10th Mountain Division, Aspen's first ski team, was placed in the plaza below the gondola lift.

Another source of civic pride was the transformation of one of Main Street's most beautiful old Victorians—the lovely old Sardy House—into an intimate luxury hotel. Built in the mining heyday, it reflected the early years of Aspen's renaissance when Tom and Alice Sardy received mourners in the front parlor (Tom

The Sardy House Christmas Tree

was the town mortician as well as the lumber yard owner, and later, the country commissioner). The same huge pine that graced the house throughout its history has become the focus of a town-wide holiday celebration when the hotel lights its Christmas tree lights.

If the restoration of historic structures became a focus for public pride, the building of the home for Prince Bandar Abdul bin Sultan, Saudi Arabia's representative to the United Nations, was a matter for much private speculation. Who could possibly need a 55,000 square foot part-time residence with 27 bathrooms? Permission to build the home took months to achieve, setting off a debate over "size" that continued for years. Some thought that the ultimate P & Z approval was influenced by the Prince's undeniable generosity to Aspen's causes; other more charitable gossips thought it was probably because absolutely no one could see the structure, which was nestled far behind the hills of McLain Flats.

But no matter how strict the zoning laws, circumstances married to allow projects that threatened some of Aspen's oldest institutions. Among them was a downtown Aspen property adjacent to the site where Aspen's life as a ski resort began—the base of the old Number One ski lift. In 1980 hotelier and wheeler-dealer Hans Cantrup gained control of the huge property at the base of Aspen Mountain, not far from his Hotel Continental.

Cantrup quickly lost the property to bankruptcy, and the ensuing owner John Roberts lost it to the infamous deal-maker Donald Trump, who lost it to Maryland developer Mohammed Hadid. Suddenly, Hadid, who was a relatively unknown to Aspenites, found himself in possession of a prime property ostensibly zoned for a 292-room hotel, by far the largest ever built in Aspen. The Ritz Carlton lost no time in stepping up to the plate as the authorized operator, making it the first downtown hotel to be affiliated with a major hotel chain.

Approval to build the Ritz Carlton took a full three years and was put to public referendums twice, drawing a record number of voters. The controversy between those who believed that the scale and the concept behind the Ritz would forever compromise Aspen and those who believed the town needed a large first-class hotel, divided the town into two adamant and angry camps. Among other things, in early 1990 the situation sparked a divisive recall election aimed at third-term mayor Bill Stirling and three of his councilmen. The mayor and two of the three councilmen survived the recall and the hotel was started. In the end, after a series of compromises concerning size, height, mass, and appearance, the Ritz Carlton opened its doors in December 1992, permanently changing the landscape, if not the opinions of those involved. Ironically, in June of 1991, Hadid himself ran out of cash and Sheik Abdul Aziz al Ibrahim, a mysterious Saudi financier, took over accounts payable and control. A short six years later, the Ritz Carlton organization proclaimed itself tired of the Sheik's "interference," and bowed out. The Sheraton stepped in and the hotel was renamed The Aspen St. Regis.

While this project was a landmark in the tug-of-war against rampant development from 1980 to the year 2000, scores of huge, multi-million dollar projects, carefully monitored by the P & Z, eventually came to fruition. The skirmishes were frequent and varied. Developers of the exclusive Wildcat Ranch, built in the midst of prime elk habitat, threw a thin bone to environmentalists by promising that homeowners would be limited to two dogs apiece; Hollywood producer Peter Guber, a prominent Hollywood producer, after being told that he could not build a second residence on his 600-acre Owl Creek ranch, was forced to tear down the new "barn" that proved to be designed for humans instead of animals.

Most developers gained control over the acres in the traditional ways. A few searched for shortcuts. Native Jim Blanning made himself famous (and eventually landed in jail) by the quiet titling of old mining claims—in other words, buying up old mining claims and then seeking out property owners who did not buy the mineral rights along with the surface rights. Then, legally, he could either demand that the current landowners pay him for the mineral rights or he would start digging in their back yards! Unfortunately, Blanning's tactics went beyond the legal, and although he protested by shouting complaints from the courthouse roof for a day and confronting the commissioners in a local bar clad in nothing but a jock strap, he eventually ended up in the hoosegow. Long-time ski instructor and would-be developer Wilk Wilkerson, quietly bought up some forty-five acres of mining claims on Smuggler Mountain, the still undeveloped hillside guarding the north side of town, and began the long struggle to populate its slopes with luxury homes. As he fought his battle for control in the courts, he also explored other tactics, such as blocking access to the mountain by rolling a gigantic boulder into the middle of the old

Smuggler Mountain Road. Unfortunately, for Wilk, the county had earthmoving equipment too.

Buzz Cooper, son of a miner, has plagued the county for over 20 years in his effort to build a home on his own claim on the back of Aspen Mountain. And Stephan Albouy, an Aspen native who grew up on the

Hillside development

slopes of Smuggler Mountain and for a time actually mined the Hyman family's Smuggler Mine, finally lost heart after years of fighting to establish a mining operation in the heart of the Maroon Bells–Snowmass Wilderness above Conundrum Creek. To some people on both sides of the growth/no growth issue, it was a life and death matter. Those who lost took it hard. Some left, and some decided to live with the changes.

Hunter Creek was another issue that brought out the passion of Aspenites from every walk of life. A rare geologic phenomenon, this spectacular hanging valley between Red Mountain and Smuggler Mountain had long been considered the town's nearby mountain playground. Blessed with spectacular views, Hunter Creek had been hosting picnickers, fishermen, and hikers since the 1880s. Suddenly, in the late 1970s, tired of parked cars that were not their own, Red Mountain homeowners blocked access via the upper entrance to the valley. Then Tom and Bonnie McCloskey, newcomers to Aspen, bought several acres at the lower entrance to Hunter Creek Valley, and after improving the southern access, made a very controversial closing of the northern access. Although the public outcry was nearly deafening, county commissioners were hard-pressed to find precedents or rulings that would or would not permit the actions of these private landowners. Meanwhile, in typical Aspen fashion, at least one family had the last laugh. In the early 1970s, long before their wealthy new neighbor set up the "No Trespassing" signs, Jim and Merilee Auster, with the stubborn fortitude of sixties' idealists, set up a spacious teepee on their mining claim in the nearly pristine Hunter Creek Valley. In the years that followed, the Austers and their two small children casually accessed their property, often on skis or snowshoes but sometimes via skidoo or jeep, on their way to and from work and school, crossing or using much disputed rights-of-way and generally driving the McCloskeys and the county crazy. And then, in 1995, just as casually, they listed their property for $7.5 million. When Auster requested an immediate $1 million cash deposit by the county to purchase the land, commissioner Mick Ireland quipped, "We're a county, not a drug cartel." But eventually it sold to the county for $2.6 million and the erstwhile hippies became millionaires.

Often the hard work and vigilance of the Historic Preservation Board and the Planning & Zoning Commission simply didn't work. In 1998, after Elizabeth Paepcke's death, the graceful family house that had been her home since the fifties was sold and, in spite of horrified local protests, torn down by the new owners. The nineteenth century home of populist governor David Waite—later occupied by Joella and Herbert Bayer—was the next historic home to fall to the wrecking ball. Officials got ready to revamp the historic preservation code making it harder for developers to change the character of the city's remaining homes. Mayor John Bennett mourned for everyone as he spoke of "our lack of stewardship."

But it was the big developments that really made a mark on the valley, especially in the late 1990s. In 1999 there were about 7,000 living units in the pipeline for building between Aspen and Glenwood Springs, making way for a potential huge influx of new residents into the Roaring Fork Valley. Among the biggest developments near Aspen were the new Aspen Highlands village, a huge residential expansion at the Aspen Business Center, and the Maroon Creek Ranch with a luxury fitness club and golf course which shared a border with the Bar Slash X Ranch, one of the last working ranches in the valley. The Pfister Ranch subdivision now cozies up to the base of Tiehack, and Horse Ranch in Snowmass brought 96 new units to the hills above Brush Creek. The Moore Family Trust, after much NIMBY (Not In My Back Yard) outcry from some of nearby Meadowwood homeowners, finally gained permission to subdivide a portion of the huge property that James Moore accumulated near the Maroon Creek junction. But they also added employee housing, a permanent structure for the cross-country team behind the schools, a new town baseball field, and continued access to the myriad of cross-country ski trails behind the public school campus.

Downvalley, the Aspen Glen Golf Course took shape near Carbondale with 128 single-family lots and 45 duplexes; Gray Ranch near Carbondale would eventually deposit close to 3,000 new homes on the remaining ranch land between Carbondale and Glenwood; and 368 residences would be built on the land that the Cerises started ranching in the 1800s. Funky and individual El Jebel, wholly owned by the Crawford family, suddenly announced that it would be subdividing the property, heretofore known chiefly for its gas station and trailer park, into land for 189 residential units, all clustered around the two-lane county road that is the primary access to the densely populated bluffs of Missouri Heights.

By the year 2000, there were nine golf courses between Aspen and Glenwood. All of them except the Aspen Golf Course, were a part of a proven formula for success—luxury homes on the links, with a view of the mountains or the river or both, and, oh yes, not too far from the very civilized amenities of Aspen's downtown.

The Cost of the Good Life

Many Aspenites, new and native, harbored a similar hope: to live a simple life in a lovely, small town. The trouble was that Walter Paepcke's original dream of a place where mind, body, and spirit would be nurtured very nearly came true, and that the combination became so desirable that everyone wanted to be a part of it. In fact, they would pay top dollar to be part of it. Before long, if you couldn't pay, you almost couldn't play.

If the cost of buying property could be called a measure of rising prices, Aspen's Board of Realtors provided annual proof. In 1992 the average

One more expensive Aspen home

price of a home was well over $1 million. This total averaged in the relatively low-cost employee units that sold for $70,000–$200,000. In 1993 the average had climbed to $1.35 million. That same year, a 3-bedroom condominium in the luxuriously renovated Collins Block downtown rented for

$7,000 a night during the two-week Christmas holiday. The Field (as in Marshall Fields) estate on Aspen Mountain, was listed for $20 million. Range Rover opened a dealership at the Aspen Business Center.

By 1994 the average price of a home in Aspen surged up to $1.75 million. In one sub-division a lot alone went for $1.74 million. That, compared to Telluride, where an intown Bed and Breakfast on five lots with an attached art gallery sold for $300,000. Commercial space downtown rose to $70–$115 per square foot, successfully edging out mom-and-pop operations and opening up space for big chain stores such as the Gap and Eddie Bauer. Costs at the local hospital were judged to be the highest in the state. Meanwhile, a study showed that the average salary of a family living in the Roaring Fork Valley was only $40,000.

In 1995, an appraisal group reported that many $1–2 million home purchases were merely "teardowns," making way for new structures. Remodeled Victorians in the West End were selling for $4–5 million. The bargains downvalley, from Aspen Village to Carbondale, were gone by the early nineties. In 1996, would-be buyers camped out to hold their place for the first 29 lots that became available at Carbondale's River Valley Ranch. In 1997, the record for real estate sales hit a high of $590 million in Pitkin County and the prices continued to rise. And up the valley in Owl Creek, until recently unpaved and practically uninhabited, a mansion sold for a record-breaking $24.8 million. The price people paid for the simple pleasures of a beautiful view in a beautiful valley!

Amenities for the Many

Aspen's beleaguered elected officials seemed to quietly agree on a single unspoken goal: to balance the inevitable advantages of the few with amenities that would improve the quality of life for the many, whether rich or poor. Many voter sponsored tax initiatives (open space, RFTA, transit tax) provided extra money for projects that the elected officials believed would benefit all of the valley's residents, both full-time and part-time.

In 1982 a city bond election approved the purchase and renovation of the Wheeler Opera House. By 1984 the lovely old sandstone building, now almost 100 years old, reopened with the accouterments needed for a modern theater hidden behind its familiar, polished, Victorian decor.

The long-argued-over Rio Grande property now boasted a large sports field, and a charming area dubbed "the Art Park." Adjacent to the Aspen Art Museum, this stubbly riverside field, long used as a snow dump by the city, was transformed by volunteers into a delightful maze of paths, flower

The new plaza next to the county courthouse

gardens, streamlets and site-specific sculptures. At the upper edge of the property was a small campus of city buildings, carefully designed to blend in with the adjacent Victorian courthouse—the parking garage, the new county library, the youth center, and the jail.

The new jail, completed in 1987, had both a view and, before long, a celebrity. The story was worthy of (and covered by) *People Magazine*. In 1991, former Indonesian first lady and international socialite Dewi Sukarno was convicted of slashing the face of her long-time rival Minnie Osmena with a broken wine glass at an Aspen soiree. Duly charged and convicted, she was sentenced to the Pitkin County jail for 60 days and to community service at the Aspen Center for Environmental Studies (ACES). She told the media that the accommodations were really very nice. ACES said that she was a good worker. The jailers merely commented on the belief that humane treatment assists in rehabilitation.

After lengthy debates and scores of suggested land-use scenarios, the school district's two downtown school buildings, deserted since 1990, were sold to the city. By 1994 the Red Brick School had been recast into offices for local non-profits and studios for local artists, with the massive gym, enhanced by a new climbing wall, preserved for another fifty years of plays, assemblies, concerts, and athletic events. The Yellow Brick School, in use since 1991 by the Early Learning Center and the Waldorf School, was finally purchased by the city in 1995. The formation of the Early Learning Center was in itself a triumph for grassroots lobbying. After years of struggling to find reasonably priced childcare solutions, Aspen's parents, backed by the city and county, started their own non-profit day-care center. It currently plays "mother" to an average of almost 100 infants and children year around.

A new library, with state-of-the-art facilities, was also opened in 1991. And to prove their dedication, its patrons formed a human chain to schlep books from one end of Main Street to the other end. Today, with 80,000 volumes, it boasts a far larger collection than cities twice its size and includes a dedicated music library originally founded in honor of a local soldier, community conference rooms, a tiny gallery, and a large collection of audio and video tapes. In 1998 a loyal card holder left $800,000 to the library to complete its upper story.

At the same time that the library, the parking garage and the new jail were completed, a luxurious youth center, partially paid for with private funds, was built as part of the Rio Grande complex. Now totally self-supporting, it hosts indoor and outdoor sports and countless activities for local and visiting young people. In 1994 the city purchased the Cozy Point Ranch at the junction of Highway 82 and Brush Creek Road, perhaps making it the only city in Colorado to own an equestrian training center. Above the library a new plaza was developed, providing fine views and plenty of space for sitters. More and better parks were also in the works. Some were funded by the Parks Association. In 1994 City Hall, the 103-year-old armory, got a $500,000 face-lift, subjecting city employees and mendicant citizens alike to a year of dust and drilling. When it was done, occupants would tell you it wasn't perfect, but another old building was preserved and continuing to serve the people.

Employee Housing and Transportation

By the year 2000, the little town of Aspen had become an acknowledged leader in the concept of creating "employee housing." Like other resort communities, its employees had essentially been priced out and thrown out. And the newly enforced commute was not the only problem: the city's youngest and most

Centennial employee housing

experimental inhabitants were just plain gone. There were no longer any funky cabins or dorm rooms, or blocks of ancient brick buildings where sub-standard rooms were filled with cheerfully stoic ski bums. As stated in the 1991 Community Plan, the "messy vitality" that was part of what made Aspen special was about to go missing.

Aspen's Housing Authority, a joint city and county body, was established in 1983, and by 1990 had either built or converted hundreds of units designed to be moderately priced which could be rented or sold only to employees with limited incomes. Furthermore, developers of free-market projects, and even individual houses, were required to add employee units or to contribute to a housing fund. New regulations prevented the destruction of old low-income housing without replacing it with an equal number of bedrooms or making a contribution to new housing. A land-use code approved by the city council in 1988 required sixty percent employee housing, and a portion of the city's tax monies were specifically allocated for the building of additional employee housing. By the year 2000 the Housing Authority, ruled by an appointed board of directors, accounted for 1,000 rental units and 800 owner units.

In spite of the employee housing projects, hundreds of Aspenites—both newcomers and old-timers—moved downvalley. The population of Basalt (20 miles from Aspen) and Carbondale (30 miles from Aspen) blossomed, as did the surrounding counties. Some who joined the downvalley movement said they preferred the quiet. Others just couldn't afford the prices or couldn't wait for an opening in employee housing. The pace was undeniably slower in the "Banana Belt" (the lower altitude brought a few weeks more of summer for wistful vegetable gardeners) and a move opened up the possibility of someday actually owning a place to live in, but it would be purchased at the price of a headache other than housing—the commute on Highway 82.

Highway 82 construction at Shale Bluffs

By the late 1970s rush-hour traffic on Highway 82 began to look like downtown Los Angeles on a two-lane road. The controversy between the state highway department and valley residents over four-laning Highway 82 had raged for over twenty years. Finally, the weary commuters won out over those who felt the valley would be ruined by a superhighway. In 1988 the Colorado Department of Transportation announced the allocation of $21 million to four-lane Highway 82. CDOT estimated that completion of the 4-lane into Aspen would take seven full years. But as commuters resigned themselves to years of highway construction delays, politicians, activists and property owners engaged in a bitter fight over just where and how the four-lane highway would enter Aspen from the west. The "Straight Shot" people advocated taking the kink out of the highway at the West End and sending the highway right into town along the old Midland Railway right-of-way. Opponents of the "Straight Shot" prepared to lay themselves down on the highway in protest. In the end, both the city and the county convinced CDOT that a "Straight Shot" would be a disaster and it was decided to end the four-lane outside of town with a right-of-way for a possible light rail to be held in abeyance for the future.

Short-term solutions to the traffic problem included: more buses traveling downvalley during commute hours; vans leased by employers to transport downvalley employees to the workplace; on Main Street a "high occupancy" lane for vehicles with two or more passengers; and at the Castle Creek/ Maroon Creek/Highway 82 intersection to the west of town, Aspen's new roundabout for the twenty-first century to facilitate traffic at this busy intersection.

As cars labored up Highway 82, and over and under every other by-way in the valley, on reaching Aspen they needed to park. Parking for visitor and resident alike became a huge problem in the eighties. Zoning soon decreed that nothing could be built without an appropriate number of parking spaces. A new parking garage, artfully hidden beneath the library and the adjacent courthouse plaza, was completed in 1990. In 1995 the City of Aspen installed European-style parking kiosks, forcing downtown drivers to cough up a fee for the privilege of nearby parking. Little notes on windshields saying "Please don't ticket me, I live here" held no sway with meter maids, and soon disappeared. So much for sentiment, said one local.

The airport, now dubbed Sardy Field after long-time commissioner Tom Sardy who championed its original building, doubled the size of the terminal in 1987 and upgraded the runway to accommodate the new numbers of private and commercial jets. In 1998 landings and take-offs totaled 45,953 of which 27,546 (60%) were by private planes. After years of having to halt landings at twilight, in 1994 Sardy Field finally got permission to land planes after dark. The airport was renovated again, improving landing capabilities and gate accommodations for the traditional two airlines that came and went from the little airport. But strangely enough, this was the one area where something went *down* in numbers. As recently as 1996 Aspen was served by four airlines; by the year 2000 Aspen and its upgraded airport facilities were used by only one regularly scheduled airline.

Throughout the ongoing auto/highway/parking problems, *almost* everyone (in Aspen "everyone" would be too much to expect) agreed that RFTA was the only thing that kept this continual-motion population sane. The

Private jets assembled at Sardy Field, the Aspen Airport

Roaring Fork Transit Authority was founded jointly by the city and county in the early eighties in an attempt to ease an already obvious problem. The concept, initially, was simple—the bus system would move people all around the immediate area (Mountain Valley on the east to Snowmass on the west) at no charge. By 1991 RFTA was moving people, bicycles and even dogs as far afield as Basalt. But nobody dreamed that less than 20 years after its founding, it would be the second largest transit system in Colorado, moving a an incredible 4 million passengers a year with daily trips to and from 40-mile distant Glenwood Springs. In-town trips are still free but dogs are no longer welcome. Such is progress.

In 1966 the train pulled out of Aspen for the last time. Ever since then, even though the tracks have long since have been pulled up to make way for the much jogged-upon Rio Grande bike and pedestrian path, train buffs have been talking about getting it back. Innumerable studies have been done, studies which show that a passenger train could and would alleviate the Highway 82 problems which will almost certainly continue well after the four-lane is completed, and studies which show that a passenger train could not possibly alleviate traffic problems. But in 1996 studies were supplanted by money and CDOT agreed to contribute $3 million towards purchase of the rail corridor right-of-way. In 1997 the Roaring Fork Holding Authority, a valley-wide coalition of three counties and five municipalities, handed over $8.5 million to take over ownership of the Denver & Rio Grande Western Corridor between Glenwood and Woody Creek. However, the debate as to whether rail was the right alternative for the valley intensified and continued into the new millennium.

Aspen's Cultural Giants

When Elizabeth and Walter Paepcke envisioned the give-and-take of great
ideas in a world filled with mountain views and magnificent music, they
could never have imagined the height to which both the Music Associates
of Aspen (MAA, the Aspen Music Festival) and the Aspen Institute would
grow. In 1991 the Joan and Irving Harris Concert Hall, a permanent re-
hearsal and performance facility holding
500 people, was completed adjacent to the
Music Festival Tent. True to its word, the
MAA began scheduling occasional winter
concerts there to feed the music-hungry
Aspenites during the winter months. During
the summer the Hall became one of the dozens of venues the MAA used for an astonishing 150 musical events; nearly 25 percent
of the events were free and, as always, seat-
ing on the lawn outside the Music Tent was
absolutely gratis, although crowded. In
1999, its 50th season, the MAA estimated
that 30,000 music lovers attended concerts
during the nine-week season and almost 900
students from 39 countries attended the Music School. With the advent of the Marolt

Irving and Joan Harris

campus housing for students, Aspenites no longer heard the strains of
practicing from nearly every available room in downtown Aspen. But the
young musicians are still everywhere, crisp in their white and black concert gear on the week-ends, and often presenting mini-concerts on the
mall, if not for much cash, at least for an audience. Friday and Sunday
concerts are so jammed that concert-goers begin arriving a hour early.
People bemoaned the loss of the old days when you cruised up to the tent
on your bicycle at the last moment and once inside the tent, spread out and
prepared to listen to world-class music in a peaceful atmosphere. "Now,"
said one amazed concert-goer, "it's like attending a refined rock concert."

In another major change, in 1999 the MAA finally announced that a permanent structure would replace the traditional music tent. It was a re-
minder that the Festival was actually run by musicians, not by corporate
functionaries. And for years, musicians, who did not appreciate the sound
of the rain drowning out a sonata, had complained about the tent acoustics.
But the majority of the Festival's audience members, many who donated
generously, loved the old tent, originally designed by Herbert Bayer with a
later version designed by architect (and Bayer's brother-in-law) Fritz Benedict. So the decision was a hard one. The new tent would be crafted from

a fabric that would still permit the play of light and shadow on the ceiling and the raising of the side panels for light and air, but the acoustics would be much improved. It was another passing of an era.

The Aspen Institute also underwent changes. After moving its headquarters to Wye on Maryland's Eastern Shore in 1980 and selling its Meadows property in the nineties, it was able to concentrate on its mission of bringing leaders together in an intellectually stimulating environment. Wye, with its proximity to Washington DC, also became the site of several high-level international gatherings, including the Wye Peace Accord in 1998 in which the U.S. brokered the peace between Israel, the PLO, and Jordan. The Institute is currently headquartered in Washington D.C., but continues to maintain its presence at the Meadows in Aspen where it holds seminars, along with periodic free lectures by some of the world's great thinkers.

The Business of Skiing

If summer, with its music, its dance, its Food and Wine Festival, its rodeos, hiking, biking, and innumerable other outdoor activities, seemed to give the world the burnish of humanities' finer achievements, winter was still filled with the rush of sheer exhilaration. Skiing—down, over, up and into—the Aspen area's spectacular mountains, was still the glue that held the town together.

By the year 2000, Aspen was a one-company town, at least where downhill skiing was concerned. In 1993, after an all-time bad year, Whip Jones, the legendary owner of the Aspen Highlands, finally threw in the towel; he turned his back on years of quarreling with his hired managers, including his son, and donated the entire ski area to Harvard University. Harvard, in turn, sold the property to Gerald Hines, a Houston millionaire, who also owned ski areas in Crested Butte and Boyne Mountain. Hines had big ideas, but most of them lay on the ground and not up the mountain. So in 1993, with his plans for a base lodge and a surrounding village well on their way, Hines sold the actual ski area to the Aspen Skiing Company for a whopping $20 million. The sale came on the heels of a banner year for the ski company in which 399,547 skier days were logged by skiers paying top dollar for ski tickets. Since then the Ski Company has completely renovated the old Merry-Go-Round restaurant halfway up the mountain, put in all new state-of-the art lifts and made the once funky Aspen Highlands into the kind of ski area that only a massive infusion of cash could create. Those who had remained loyal to the Highlands over the years—reveling in the low-cost lift ticket, the less crowded slopes, the unbelievable rush of the run down Loges Peak, and an atmosphere where everyone knew each other—knew they had lost something irreplaceable. But, as those realistic former ski bums would be the first to tell you, life moves on.

Almost from its genesis, the Aspen Skiing Company, for many years with the indomitable D. R. C. Brown at its helm, was embroiled in one controversy or another. It was a business, first and foremost. And it was often at odds with both environmentalists—who decried expansion if it encroached on animal migration routes and potential wilderness land—and with the no-growth advocates who feared the effects of more and more people arriving to ski on more and more territory. After several years of elections

The new base area at Aspen Highlands under construction

and public forums, the Aspen Skiing Company finally had its way with Burnt Mountain, whose untouched hillsides flowed down beside the area's Elk Creek slopes. On the valley floor below, Two Creeks provided an entirely new access to the Snowmass Ski Area. Environmentalists had lost another battle. However, the Skiing Company worked at adapting to the climate and in December 1997 started the Environment Foundation and launched a number of environmental initiatives, including a wind-powered ski lift on the Cirque at Snowmass. And though a 1998 study showed that Aspen had come close to having a true, year-round economy, the ski industry was still the economic backbone.

So, with a lift ticket price that was consistently the highest in the United States and with record-breaking skier days, the Skiing Company continued to upgrade all of their slopes and all of their facilities. Numerous high-speed quads went in at all the mountains, and new restaurants replaced those that a generation had grown up with. Season passes were scanned by a machine instead of by a human being. And in 1999 work began on the new $14 million Sundeck atop Aspen Mountain, complete with sit-down dining, a much enlarged cafeteria and, a la Zermatt and St. Moritz, a "private" mountain-top club with a restaurant that would seat

200 and have nighttime access via the gondola. Snowboarding was recognized as the wave of the future and the Skiing Company created a lift ticket just for riders. Aspen Mountain still remains off limits for snowboarders, but two halfpipes and three terrain parks have been created at Snowmass, one halfpipe and one terrain park is offered at Buttermilk, and riders are welcomed at Aspen Highlands.

The ever business-like Aspen Skiing Company did lose a few skirmishes over the decade. Weary of the chaos created by the annual Roche Cup race, a part of the World Cup circuit, the Skiing Company announced in 1995 that it would not play host the following year. Vail quickly snapped up the prize and by 1996 the Skiing Company had changed its mind. It wanted the race back. The Roche Cup came back, but the beancounters had the last word; the World Cup volunteers, who put in hundreds of hours producing the race, would no longer receive the much coveted World Cup ski jacket and free lift tickets.

Although the new drug-testing of employees continues to be mandatory, the Skiing Company backed down on their announcement that no male employees could have pony tails or goatees, and that neither men nor women could have noserings or more than one earring per ear. Unseen body piercing was not mentioned. And when the Skiing Company, in an effort to change Buttermilk's beginner-slope image, announced that the entire Buttermilk/Tiehack area would now be known simply as Tiehack, the locals revolted. History proved too strong for the Skiing Company and the name was changed back to the traditional Buttermilk Mountain.

But lest it be painted as a corporation without a sentimental bone in its 50+-year old body, in honor of the millennium celebration, the Aspen Skiing Company offered $39/day lift tickets and other specials for early season purchasers. It was a far cry from the free season pass that ever bona fide town employee got in the late 1960s, but it was a gesture. As was the Aspen Valley Ski Club, a non-profit organization, originally heavily subsidized by the Skiing Company, for the valley school children. For a few hundred dollars a season, children, with student ski passes, could attend full-day Club ski classes taught by Aspen Skiing Company instructors for nearly every Saturday and Sunday of the ski season. For many parents it made the whole struggle of raising a family in the Roaring Fork Valley worthwhile, and rescued the much maligned Skiing Company from its sometimes venal reputation.

The Aspen Character

Years before Aspen was what it is, Fritz Benedict and Walter and Elizabeth Paepcke and Friedl Pfeifer and Mary Hayes and Stuart Mace and Bil Dunaway and the tough-minded natives who stuck out the poverty of the quiet years, and perhaps the miners before them, were people of character. They seemed to believe that Aspen was a place where a man or a woman could carve out a life without compromise. It was, and in many ways still is, a world of individuals. Everyone, to the pleasure or the frustration of everyone else, has an opinion. But whatever Aspen is, Aspen didn't get there by accident, as one historian put it. "Right or wrong, we thought it up and we made it happen."

Fritz Benedict

Mary Eshbaugh Hayes

Aside from all the battles over growth and zoning, in keeping with the litigiousness nature of Aspen's citizens, other controversial issues were frequently brought before the city council or the commissioners by residents who hoped to make their own personal passions into law. The forerunner of lifestyle lawmaking was the banning of billboards along Highway 82 in the sixties. It's a law that still stands. Soon after, setting the tone for the esthetics of Aspen's nightscape, neon lights were banned. In 1985 Aspen had become one of the first communities in the country to forbid smoking in restaurants. Its hospital was the first in the nation to test all surgery candidates for HIV and to reserve the right to test trauma victims who could not sign permission slips. Rather than risk piecemeal designation, Aspen's entire downtown was declared a Historic Preservation District, again preventing the blight that affected so many other old mining towns and preserving the nineteenth century charm that still clings to the brick facades of Wheeler's city.

Stuart Mace

Controversial fur sales in Aspen

Other harbingers of change announced themselves in the late 1980s, and again sparked years of debate. Should there be dogs on buses? Was a bikini contest contrary to the spirit of Winterskol? Should the Owl Creek road be paved? Should there be a path across the wetlands? A few revolutionary laws were foiled in 1989 and 1990 when the anti-fur lobby tried to pass a law prohibiting the sale of furs in Aspen. Environmentalists also tried for a prohibition against the sale of ivory, but that effort reached little more than the newspapers.

Even the Federal government had to give in to Aspen's fighting spirit occasionally. In the late eighties, when the EPA insisted that it needed to tear up acres of lower Smuggler Mountain, displacing hundreds of families, a tribe of naysayers led by an outraged housewife eventually proved the project unnecessary and forced them to back down. (The "housewife" went on to be a county commissioner). And in the late nineties, when a new-broom postmaster banned the many newspaper racks at the post office and reversed the traffic pattern, the postmaster general received so many complaints that the newspaper racks and the old traffic pattern were reinstalled. Little did the new postmaster realize that he had gone up against a time-honored Aspen tradition: the exchange of gossip, in person and via the printed word, at the Aspen post office.

As might be expected, right into the new century, among Aspenites new and old, there was no shortage of opinions. Freedom of expression, always a revered Aspen privilege, was still alive and well. And while the very character of Aspen's independent citizens may forever prevent true consensus, at least the essential element of the traditional Aspenite remained unchanged—the right to fight for whatever belief the individual held most dear. At the end of the twentieth century, just as in the nineteenth century, everyone had a different opinion, but everyone still cared.

Bil Dunaway

The character of life in Aspen changed. Some longtime locals simply grew weary of the rising costs and life-style wars and moved elsewhere. Others noted that despite the problems, they still hadn't found anyplace better to live. But one not-so-young local dressed in not-so-new ski clothes recently said it best. As he shouldered his skis under brilliant sunshine and a brilliant blue sky, he glanced at the waiting slopes of Aspen Mountain, grinned and said, "Life's tough in paradise, ain't it?" and headed off for another perfect day. ✒

Bibliography

Aspen Times. *Year in Review. 1991–1998.*

Bancroft, Caroline. *Famous Aspen.* The Golden Press, 1954.

Clifford, Peggy. *Aspen: Dreams & Dilemmas.* The Swallow Press, Inc., 1970.

_____. *To Aspen and Back.* St. Martin's Press, 1980.

Hyman, Sidney. *The Aspen Idea.* Norman: University of Oklahoma Press, 1975.

Landry, Janet, and Joan Lane. *"Horsethief" Kelley and His Camera.* 1972

Markalunas, Jim. *Aspen, The Quiet Years. 1910-1930.*

Marshall, Jamie, ed. *The Aspens.* The aspen Skiing Company, 1989.

O'Rear, John and Frankie. *The Aspen Story.* A. S. Barnes, 1966.

Pearce, Sarah J., and Roxanne Eflin. *Aspen and the Roaring Fork Valley.* Cordillera Press, Inc., 1990.

Rohrbough, Malcom J. *Aspen, the History of a Silver Mining Town.* Oxford Press, 1986.

Sterling, Martha Whitcomb. *Oh Be Joyful! An Historic Tale of the Aspen Silver Camp.* 1975

_____. *The Historical Hotel Jerome.* 1986.

Vertical files. Archives, Aspen Historical Society, Aspen, Colorado.

Wentworth, Frank L. *Aspen on the Roaring Fork.* Sundance Limited, 1976.

Notes

1. Peggy Clifford, *To Aspen and Back,* 22.

2. Clifford, *Aspen: Dreams & Dilemmas,* 150.

3. Clifford, *To Aspen and Back,* 94.

Index